OUTSTANDING AGAINST THE ODDS
Lessons from Exceptional Primary School Leaders

BY SONIA GILL, JO SAVIDGE,
HELEN NICHOLSON, PAUL MURPHY,
MAXINE LOW, BETH DYER,
PAULA PHILIPS, IAN SCOTCHBROOK

Although every effort has been made to ensure that website addresses are correct at time of going to press, Hachette Learning cannot be held responsible for the content of any website mentioned in this book. It is sometimes possible to find a relocated web page by typing in the address of the home page for a website in the URL window of your browser.

Hachette UK's policy is to use papers that are natural, renewable and recyclable products and made from wood grown in well-managed forests and other controlled sources. The logging and manufacturing processes are expected to conform to the environmental regulations of the country of origin.

To order, please visit www.HachetteLearning.com or contact Customer Service at education@hachette.co.uk / +44 (0)1235 827827.

ISBN: 978 1 0360 0736 2

© Sonia Gill 2025

First published in 2025 by
Hachette Learning,
An Hachette UK Company
Carmelite House
50 Victoria Embankment
London EC4Y 0DZ
www.HachetteLearning.com

The authorised representative in the EEA is Hachette Ireland, 8 Castlecourt Centre, Dublin 15, D15 XTP3, Ireland (email: info@hbgi.ie)

Impression number   10 9 8 7 6 5 4 3 2 1

Year   2029 2028 2027 2026 2025

All rights reserved. Apart from any use permitted under UK copyright law, no part of this publication may be reproduced or transmitted in any form or by any means, electronic or mechanical, including photocopying and recording, or held within any information storage and retrieval system, without permission in writing from the publisher or under licence from the Copyright Licensing Agency Limited. Further details of such licences (for reprographic reproduction) may be obtained from the Copyright Licensing Agency Limited, www.cla.co.uk

Cover photo © Yuliya Derbisheva VLG / shutterstock.com

Illustrations by DC Graphic Design Limited, Hextable, Kent.

Typeset in the UK.

Printed in the UK.

A catalogue record for this title is available from the British Library.

Acknowledgements

I would like to extend a huge thank you to all of the headteachers who have taken the time to contribute to this book. Their chapters are only the tip of the iceberg, because they are the result of years of dedication and hard work for their children, teams and communities. Thank you also for the privilege of being on your school's journeys – you constantly inspire.

Thank you to James Page for writing the foreword to this book and being my 'go to' boost when it feels like striving for excellence is impossible.

To Georgia and the Clio and Write Business Results teams, this book has been in my head for a long time, but I couldn't work out how to make it a reality until Clio was born. And thank you to Kat, our editor who has been utterly amazing to work with and was instrumental in bringing this book together.

To my husband Phil, who gets all the behind-the-scenes highs and lows and keeps me on track.

And finally, thank you to Alex and the team at John Catt publishing for their ongoing support for my work and that of many educators.

Dedication

This book is dedicated to all headteachers and school leaders, and everyone in education who works tirelessly to give their children the very best education.

Your job is both joyful and relentless, but you are the magic makers of the future.

Your commitment and dedication to the lives of your children, as well as your teams and communities, shines bright.

We don't thank you enough.

We don't resource you well enough.

But somehow you find a way to shine.

Not many people could do what you do.

Stay brilliant, because you are outstanding against the odds.

Contents

Acknowledgements iii
Dedication iv
Foreword vi
Introduction viii
Chapter 1: Why do so many schools get to 'good' but not 'outstanding'? – Sonia Gill 1
Chapter 2: The power of culture – Jo Savidge 13
Chapter 3: No-excuses culture – Helen Nicholson 39
Chapter 4: The transformation journey – Paul Murphy 61
Chapter 5: From challenges to opportunities – Maxine Low 83
Chapter 6: Using inspections as catalysts – Beth Dyer 105
Chapter 7: Cultivating a high-performing team – Paula Philips 123
Chapter 8: Nurturing an exceptional school culture – Ian Scotchbrook 147
Conclusion 167
Connect with the authors 170

Foreword

This is a book that needs to be read by educators and school leaders across the sector. It hardly needs to be stated just how challenging the context is in schools: there is no money, buildings are creaking, there is a recruitment and retention emergency, and children and families are under more pressure than ever after the Covid-19 pandemic with the cost of living crisis.

And yet. In *Outstanding Against the Odds*, Sonia Gill and the inspiring school leaders who have worked closely with Heads Up show that the truly exceptional is still possible with empowering leadership and a focus on building the right culture.

Sonia has spent over a decade walking into recently 'outstanding' schools (probably more than anyone else!), researching what makes the difference, learning from these improvement journeys and distilling the fundamentals. Excellence (and achieving 'outstanding') must remain a positive and energising goal, ensuring that reduced expectations do not quietly and perniciously take hold as the pressures across education continue.

At Haringey Education Partnership, we have worked extremely closely with some of the schools featured in this book as well as many more that have achieved sustained and profound improvement through working with Heads Up. As a result, I know the real impact this can make. Heads Up also has a powerful track record of the schools they support being far more likely to get 'outstanding'.

As Paul Murphy reflects in 'the transformation rollercoaster' (see page 61), the journey is not likely to be a simple one or linear. But making the school vision, values and direction explicit, built around high ambition for the children and the school, followed up with consistent leadership and behaviours to not only talk the talk but walk the walk, makes a powerful difference which grows cumulatively over time. Constant attention to these fundamentals actually makes leading significantly easier too, with everyone pointing in the same direction and distributing the load, with the whole team and school community contributing more than the sum of the parts.

While intangible, the culture set by leaders makes a very recognisable impact with measurable outcomes. And, as Ian Scotchbrook reflects (see page 147), this is picked up by staff, parents and anyone (including inspectors) who enters your school.

I hope you enjoy reading the book as much as I have, and take on board both Sonia's wisdom and the real-life journeys and insights these school leaders have shared with such honesty and integrity.

James Page
Chief Executive, Haringey Education Partnership

Introduction

If you've picked up this book, we imagine you are a headteacher or senior leader in a primary school in the UK who is looking for some ideas about how to make your school outstanding. As headteachers ourselves, we know the challenges you face, as we have likely encountered many of the same ones.

Being an educator, and a school leader, is proving to be difficult in the 21st century. We are facing ever-accelerating levels of change within the world around us as well as in the education system. Technology is advancing more rapidly than we can teach about it. Climate change is a genuine threat. Disinformation can spread faster than ever. A global pandemic with its long tail continues to affect our schools and has emphasised the complex needs of our children. And we have fewer resources to meet all these challenges than we have had over the last decade.

You and your team still show up steadfastly every day because you are united by your passion to give all your pupils the best possible start in life. This does not only include providing an academic education; you want to equip the pupils you lead with the skills they'll need to support their emotional and social wellbeing long into the future.

But despite its importance, this is not something that's assessed by Ofsted. The pressures of the school inspection system can sometimes make us feel as though we are ticking boxes. What we hope to show you through our stories and experiences is that you *can* deliver the holistic level of education you want for your pupils *and* meet Ofsted's inspection criteria.

We've found that focusing on the underlying culture in your school is often what makes such holistic education possible and is the difference between receiving a 'good' rating and an 'outstanding' one.

At the time of publication, we know the Ofsted and inspection framework have rightly been under intense scrutiny. Recently we have seen welcome, positive and much needed changes and there are more to come. Maybe 'outstanding' will no longer be a term used to refer to schools. And that's okay, because the real-life stories shared here are about excellence in education, whatever shorthand we use to describe it.

Who are we?

The majority of the contributors to this book are headteachers at schools that are considered to have the odds stacked against them. None of us view our schools purely through this lens – we see pupils who are keen to learn and staff who are ready to deliver the education our children deserve. We are very aware of the challenges we face in our schools, and although on paper you could say we face challenging circumstances that are beyond our control, none of us have let that stop us or our teams from doing our best every single day. Is it tough? Yes. Would we change our pupils or communities? Not for the world.

As you'll see throughout the book, our challenges include having a higher than the national average number of students with special educational needs (SEND) or with a SEND Education, Health and Care Plan (EHCP). Some of us have schools with a higher number of pupils than the national average for whom English is not their first language, and others have more pupils who are eligible for free school meals than the national average.

While this data gives an indication of the challenges we may face, it is far from the whole picture. Our hope is that what we share in this book will give you a new perspective on school leadership and help you to see how, regardless of the challenges you currently face, it is possible not only to turn things around but to help your pupils and staff achieve more – perhaps more than they currently believe is possible – without working even harder than you already do.

The importance of culture in moving from good to great

What all of us have learned in our time as headteachers is that our schools' cultures are the common denominator for delivering excellence. This has meant building a strong cultural ecosystem, which is not a quick fix – it takes time, buy-in and effort from everyone on your team and the wider school community. But when you get this right, you'll see your pupils' progress accelerate, build a happier and more productive team of staff and create a community that supports and recognises what you provide.

What headteacher doesn't want that? There are several elements that make up a cultural ecosystem, and we'll discuss each of them in the chapters throughout this book. Broadly, they can be split into three areas: the vision for your school, the values your school believes in and how those are represented by behaviour, and the strategies you use to roll out your vision and values. When all three of these elements are in place and working together, the results are outstanding.

The journey we'll go on in this book

We'll begin our journey together with Sonia, who will discuss what schools can do to move from 'good' to 'outstanding' and why so many get stuck at 'good'. From there, we'll explore the power of school culture with Jo. Helen introduces us to the no-excuses culture she embedded with great success in her school, and then Paul explores what it means to go on a successful transformation journey.

Maxine brings in her unique approach to problem solving and innovation within schools and shares how we can take lessons from the business world, while Beth discusses how to use Ofsted inspections as catalysts to drive change and how to make the process more valuable than it is stressful. Next, Paula focuses on what it means to cultivate a high-performing team and shows how valuable that is for developing and maintaining your culture of excellence. Finally, Ian discusses how we can sustain an exceptional culture once we've created it.

We hope you find what we share in these pages useful and inspiring. Are you ready to be part of the movement to make all our schools outstanding?

Chapter 1:
Why do so many schools get to 'good' but not 'outstanding'? – Sonia Gill

Sonia Gill is an educational leadership coach and the founder and director of Heads Up. With over a decade of experience working with school leaders and as a former primary school teacher, Sonia has a deep understanding of the challenges and pressures facing primary schools and their leadership teams in the UK. She is passionate about making every school outstanding for both the children and communities they serve. For Sonia, the Ofsted rating is a byproduct and not a goal in itself, though the schools Sonia and her team support are significantly more likely to gain or maintain the 'outstanding' judgement.

I was a teacher. I'd worked full-time, as a supply teacher and as a specialist intervention teacher with gifted and talented pupils, and those with borderline GCSE pass grades; I'd worked in primary, secondary and special settings, while also deciding to explore other avenues. I was excited to then be selected by the John Lewis leadership programme and spent many happy years in the partnership. John Lewis sells stuff (rather nice stuff, I think), and yet they were focused on their people, culture and high performance. As a psychology graduate, these were things that had always fascinated me.

Despite being in retail, I kept looking at education and wondering, why? Why do so many schools become 'good' and stay there – which is no small feat – but so few go on to become outstanding? It went from being a general wondering to a nagging question I couldn't shake.

> So, in 2011 I left John Lewis and set out to understand what outstanding schools look like and why so many stop at 'good'. My guiding questions were:
> - Were these so-called 'outstanding' schools really any better than other schools?
> - If they are, what were they doing differently?
>
> What could we learn from the best schools – if indeed they were 'the best' – to help other schools achieve the same? I know that as educators we all want the best for our pupils, so this became my mission. It's what led me to where I am today, and to writing this book with many wonderful headteachers I've met on my journey to uncover what lies behind 'outstanding'.

My learning journey

I'd like to say I embarked on this journey of discovery unbiased, but I was sceptical. I'd read the stories and heard the rumblings that I'm sure you've also heard, such as:

- 'Outstanding schools aren't really any better than good schools.'
- 'They become "outstanding" by hot-housing their children, off-rolling them or through other nefarious means.'
- They have unhappy staff, who burn out and leave.

I'm happy to say that my scepticism proved unfounded. I believe there is plenty to learn from any and all schools, because there is so much great practice, innovation and dedication in our classrooms. However, time is limited for all of us, so I set two criteria to determine which of the over 30,000 UK schools I would visit:

1. **The school had to be recently 'outstanding' (within the last 12 months).** This was particularly important as at the time 'outstanding' schools were not subject to reinspection, something which I'm glad has changed.
2. **They had to have tough demographics.** I thought if these schools could create a genuinely outstanding culture despite additional challenges to those facing schools nationally at any given time, then wow!

I've never stopped learning from these schools. For over a decade, I've been walking into recently 'outstanding', 'good' and 'requires improvement' schools, trying to understand what outstanding schools were doing differently, if anything.

What did I find?

1. They really were outstanding.
2. They weren't doing anything 'dodgy' to get there (with the exception of two schools).
3. They had the happiest teams I'd ever met, who were often working fewer hours than those in good schools.

And many, many times my heart would swell, and I'd have to fight back the tears of joy as I looked at the stunning, holistic, whole-person education that was being delivered. It really was outstanding.

I'm not saying those headline-grabbing, not-really-outstanding, horrible-to-their-teams schools don't exist, but I've struggled to find them. I keep thinking about beliefs regarding outstanding schools, and I find most are wrong. From 2022 to 2023, my team researched five assumptions about outstanding schools:

1. Is it impossible to maintain 'outstanding'? **No.**
2. Is it easier for 'outstanding' schools because they exist in areas with easier demographics? **No.**
3. Do they get better results? **Yes.**
4. Do they have fewer pupils who require additional support? **No.**
5. Do they have more money than other schools? **Yes, but only because they tend to be 15% larger than the average school.**

You can find the full report here: ukheadsup.com/outstanding-myths/

What was the difference in outstanding schools?

I looked and listened hard. I still do. I wanted to find that magic 'one thing', the quick win or clickbait we all hope will make life easier. I considered the following factors:

- Was it a particular approach?
- A certain scheme of work?
- An approach to behaviour?
- The length of experience of a headteacher?
- Stable staff?
- Experienced staff?
- New staff?
- Money?
- Resources?
- Local talent pool?
- Parental engagement?

None of these factors were consistent across the schools. I found every variation.

But there was one consistent thing: culture. Everyone is totally on board with what the school wants to achieve, and they are doing what needs to be done.

Don't get me wrong, these aren't utopias. But these schools have high team alignment, and a team fired up about the school's vision and plan to achieve it. In contrast to other schools, it means they don't have to chase consistency, certainly not as much, and it doesn't feel like – to quote some headteachers I know – 'herding cats' or 'trying to stick jelly to the wall'.

Good schools have good policies and practices in place, but not everyone is adhering to them. This is the difference between good and great – people. You can have the policies and processes in place, but if these aren't followed by everyone then they don't create the greatest possible impact. Outstanding schools have everyone on board and proactively make sure they continue to do so, which means they are able to take their practice and drive it further forward. The teams at these schools can invest energy in fine tuning what they are doing because they are all doing what needs to be done, not through policing (management) but through their culture (leadership).

The cultural ecosystem provides clarity

You're going to hear a lot about culture, vision and values in this book. This is because they have been a key part of schools' journeys to 'outstanding', and I would say they are key features of almost all outstanding schools.

Is the school culture the 'one thing'? No. We all know there isn't one thing that makes a school outstanding. But it's an aspect that can cause confusion for many of us. In my experience, we either don't realise we have a school culture issue, or we are not sure what the cultural ecosystem is. Let's look at each in turn.

We don't realise we have a school culture issue

I'd like to share an activity I've done with many heads and have seen a lot of light bulbs go on as a result. It involves some simple maths.

1. How many people are in your team (payroll)?
2. How many of them are superstars? You know these people, they're brilliant. Totally aligned with your culture, they do a great job. If you could clone them, you would!
3. How many people are there some 'issues' with? You know these people as well. No one comes to work to do a bad job, but some people are just a bit tricky, or don't do their job very well for whatever reason.
4. And now, how many people are left (i.e. the number of people on payroll minus the superstars and the people with some 'issues')? These are solidly good people.

I find it helpful to put these numbers in the following diagram. Feel free to work out the percentages.

Number of team members (payroll):_____		
Superstars	Solid team members	Team members where we have 'issues'

Where are the majority of people?

I've asked so many heads this question, and what I've found is:

- The majority at the top (superstars) = outstanding school.
- The majority in the middle (solid) = good school.
- The majority at the bottom (some issues) = less than good school.

In most schools, the majority are in the middle – and we know most schools are good. The reason we don't realise we have a school culture issue is because when the majority of people are in the middle, nothing is really broken or bad. It's the reason schools get stuck at good and it's not a problem unless you want to be performing better.

Take a moment to think about your numbers:

- What if everyone at the bottom (typically around 10% in good schools) moved up or off (in the nicest way – I'm a fan of leaving with love)? How much of a difference would this make to your school? Sit with that for a moment.
- Usually there are 40-80% in the middle. What if even half of those in the middle moved up to the top? How much of a difference would that make? Again, sit with that for a moment.

I love watching headteachers glow as they think about how having a team that is much more aligned and on board would make such a difference. Maybe you're feeling that too? Whatever your numbers tell you, there is always a way to move forward.

Simple strategies for success

I'll briefly touch on what I've found is the best strategy, depending on where the majority of your team is.

- **The majority at the top (superstars) = outstanding school.** Accelerate excellence – this is about surrounding yourself and your team with high performers, because it can be hard to find that stretch.
- **The majority in the middle (solid) = good school.** Align the team – this is about creating your cultural ecosystem so that your team becomes high performing.
- **The majority at the bottom (some issues) = less than good school.** Address issues – this is where we need to get really good at having difficult conversations in a kind and effective way.

In this chapter, we're going to look more at how we can align the team, because this is where the transformational shift happens. Many of the heads who have contributed to this book will share their experiences of aligning their teams and creating strong cultures. However, if you know you have some issues to solve, you may find my book, *Successful Difficult Conversation in School*, helpful.

What is the cultural ecosystem?

A 'cultural ecosystem' is made up of three parts:

1. **Strategy** – which outlines our path (plan) to the goal.
2. **Values** – which define who we are and how we behave.
3. **Vision** – which articulates our purpose.

They have distinct and interlocking roles.

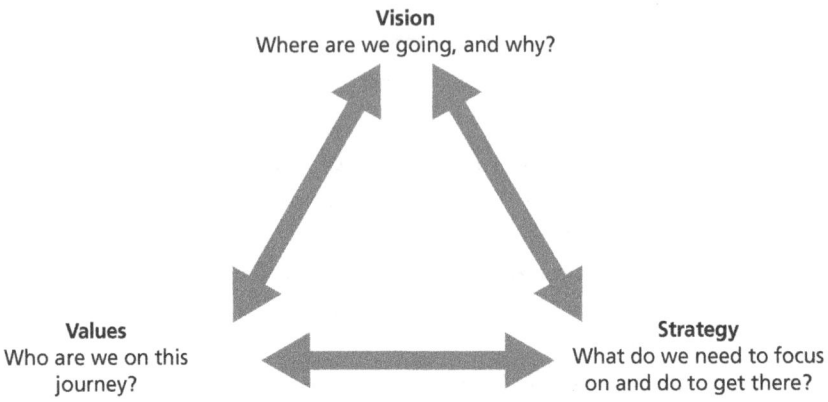

You're probably thinking, 'We have all of those', but as with so many things, the difference between a good and a great ecosystem lies in the quality of each component and how it is embedded in the school.

At times you may have felt frustrated that not everyone has bought into your vision, mission or ethos statement, and that's understandable. When you're trying so hard to move the needle in these areas it can be hard to see what else you could do. However, leaders are often not taught how to create even just a powerful vision, let alone this cultural ecosystem. And herein lies the problem.

The cultural ecosystem is not a 'nice to have' – it is essential if we want to unlock high performance in our teams. All three elements of the cultural ecosystem are important, but I find that the level of buy-in a team has around a school's vision is a good way to gauge how good or great a school's culture currently is. When it's working well, this ecosystem provides clarity that runs far deeper than policies and non-negotiables ever can.

Don't misunderstand me: policies and non-negotiables are useful tools that are trying to achieve the same goal of alignment and consistency. But, in my experience, they don't work as well as a fully formed cultural ecosystem because they are management tools. It's a bit like trying to dig a trench with a trowel – progress will be slow and hard work. Sometimes you just need a bigger spade, or even a digger, to move the earth quicker and with less effort. Culture is your 'digger'. Creating a strong cultural ecosystem requires greater people leadership tools than policies and non-negotiables, and this is what we need if we're to move from good to great.

The buy-in rate for schools' visions is not as high as you may expect. I've asked over 1000 school leaders this question: 'What percentage of your team remember your vision?' And when I say 'remember', I don't mean the team can chant it; I mean they consistently use it to inform their actions.

Here are the results (NB due to rounding, the combined percentages exceed 100%):

Up to 20%	27%	
Up to 40%	29%	95%
Up to 60%	23%	
Up to 80%	16%	
Up to 90%	5%	6%
100%	1%	

As you can see, the vast majority of schools have no more than 80% of their team's buy-in, with a significant number at either 60% or 40%. A very small number reach a 90% buy-in rate. However, when a powerful vision is created and communicated well, the buy-in rate can reach around 95%. When you reach this level of buy-in, people are visibly moved, motivated and up for the challenge that the vision sets out.

It's worth noting that when you've got a low percentage of people who are buying in – 20%, 40%, 60%, even 80% – the conversation should not be about *them* not buying in; it needs to focus on *why* there's a lack of buy-in. In almost all cases, it's because we haven't done the job we need to as leaders: creating that powerful vision and communicating it well as part of the cultural ecosystem.

Now, if you're thinking, 'I've really tried to do this and I've worked so hard', don't give yourself a hard time. As leaders, we're all told the importance of vision, but most of us have not been trained in how to create a powerful one. In fact, I've asked over 1000 school leaders, and 82% can't say with confidence that they have been shown how to create a powerful vision.

So, how do you create a powerful, compelling vision? In this book there are many examples of how heads have got their culture right through their vision and values, which means their strategies work better. Strategy is often the most developed part of the ecosystem, but if few people are delivering it well, we don't get the great results we could.

> When I was at John Lewis, I was on a fast-track leadership scheme. This meant I moved jobs often. In every new job I was asked what my vision was. I wasn't sure – was it to keep customers and partners happy? That sounded okay, but it lacked something and never seemed to be quite right.
>
> I was asked so many times that I started to wonder if I'd missed a memo or some training about vision because I clearly wasn't getting this right! Did I need to lie in a floatation tank, with aromatherapy and whale songs, and wait for this vision to arrive? It turns out no, and over time I learned not only how to create a powerful vision but also how to put in place the cornerstones of the cultural ecosystem so that teams could move from good to great. These are just some of the tools I now share with the heads I work with.

I'm not going to go into depth about how to create a powerful vision – not because I'm holding out on you, but because you can find out more about that in my book, *Journey to Outstanding* (2nd edition). I'd only be repeating myself here.

This book, *Outstanding Against the Odds*, brings to life examples from heads like you who are facing all the national challenges you face, and many local challenges too, and have found a way to deliver outstanding education.

Inspiration for the journey to 'outstanding'

What I hope this book gives you is not the headline-grabbing stories of some outstanding school that isn't really outstanding, or a school that lost that judgement, but the stories of wonderful people like you who want to create the very best education, who have wrestled with challenge after challenge and succeeded, as you will too.

This isn't the end of their journey. Right now, these heads are all in their schools working hard and dealing with challenges, just as you are.

For them, as I imagine is the case for you – and is for me too – none of this work was ever about Ofsted. It's not a perfect system, which Beth Dyer covers this really well in chapter 6. But it's the system we have to work within.

I adore each and every one of these heads. I've had the honour of working with all of them, helping some get their cultural ecosystem in place and supporting others on the journey beyond outstanding. I'm in awe of what they have accomplished with their schools. Yes, it's been hard work for them, but you know that running a school is hard work even when it's going well! So, if it's hard work regardless, let's make that hard work create a genuinely outstanding school for children – not Ofsted – and use your hard work to achieve more, with more fun.

I hope you're inspired to do all that and more by what you read in the following chapters. I hope you visit these schools yourself; I know the heads would welcome you. Go and see how amazing these schools are, how happy the teams are and how wonderful the education that is being provided is. They are genuinely outstanding, despite the odds!

Chapter 2:
The power of culture – Jo Savidge

Meet Jo...

Jo Savidge has been the headteacher of Clockhouse Primary School since 2013, having joined the school in 2004 as a teacher. She has taken it on, in her words, 'a bumpy road to outstanding' during her tenure, from 'requires improvement' to 'outstanding'. When she took on the headship, she knew she had to get the culture right. By focusing on culture first, Jo and her team have created an incredible school with strong links to its community that makes a significant difference to the lives of the children they serve.

About Clockhouse Primary School

	School	National average
Pupils with a SEND Education, Health and Care Plan	3.1%	2.5%
Pupils with SEND support	8.2%	13.5%
Pupils whose first language is not English	19.2%	22.0%
Pupils eligible for free school meals at any time during the past six years	29.4%	25.9%

> I never set out to be a headteacher, despite both my parents and my grandmother having been headteachers. When I told my mum that I'd been asked to become acting head at Clockhouse Primary, and that I'd love to get the school to 'outstanding', she had only one question for me: 'What have you got to do to get there?'
>
> I replied, 'I've got to change the culture.'
>
> In this chapter, I'll share with you how we did that at Clockhouse Primary and explain what worked for us, so you can explore whether taking similar steps will work in your school.

In at the deep end

I still vividly remember the day my headteacher told me she was leaving the school. It was a Friday afternoon in January 2013. Her announcement that she was looking for jobs in London hit me like a bolt from the blue. As deputy head, I suddenly felt like I'd been cast adrift.

Within months, the governors had asked me to become acting head. I can still picture the day they handed me the keys to the head's office. I unlocked the door, walked into the room and sat at the desk, staring at the wall. 'What now?' was the only thought running around my head.

I was in the middle of my National Professional Qualification for Headship. I had three people stepping into senior leadership posts for the first time. Handing me the keys to the head's office felt like a case of 'over to you', and I felt that everyone was watching me.

At the time of publication, we have 740 children at our school, a parent population of well over 1000 and over 100 staff. You can see a snapshot of our pupil demographics at the beginning of this chapter – it's very mixed. We have many parents who have no university experience, and many who are unemployed. Many have only ever lived in Collier Row, Romford.

Due in part to the additional resource provision for autistic children, which opened in 2017, we have many children with an Education, Health and Care Plan, both in the provision and in the main school. We also have many children with SEND support who are part of the mainstream student body. Our borough in London certainly isn't the easiest place to grow up.

> One school residential trip from several years ago has always stuck in my mind. We were driving on the M25 when one child said, 'What's this road, miss? It's very big!'
>
> This highlighted to me how many of our children don't really get out of Collier Row. We have gun crime, prostitution, drug abuse and many other challenges within our community. Just when I think something new can't come along, it always does...

The first 'call'

Six months into my headship, I felt incredibly worried that Ofsted may call. I was so concerned about it that I spoke to my school improvement partner. They reassured me that, as it had only been two years and three months since the school's previous Ofsted inspection, I had time.

Of course, the very next day the Ofsted call came. We had nothing – not even a proper self-evaluation form or a school improvement plan. I'd been fighting fires since I stepped up. To put it bluntly, we were a mess. The lead inspector was a force to be reckoned with and the inspection was really hard and upsetting. My staff kept telling me they were behind me, and that it was okay, but I felt anything but okay at the time.

As I'd expected we didn't do well, and we became a 'requires improvement' (RI) school following that inspection.

Clockhouse Primary School

Clockhouse Lane, Collier Row, Romford, Essex, RM5 3QR

Inspection dates	6–7 February 2014	
Overall effectiveness	Requires improvement	3
Achievement of pupils	Requires improvement	3
Quality of teaching	Requires improvement	3
Behaviour and safety of pupils	Good	2
Leadership and management	Requires improvement	3
Overall effectiveness at previous inspection	Good	2

We were broken in so many ways, and it felt like the worst time. However, with hindsight I can see that it was the best thing that could have happened to our school, because it set us on the journey that's brought us to where we are today. In 2014, the woman who never intended to become a headteacher, let alone the headteacher at Clockhouse Primary, had to roll up her sleeves and start somewhere. We've never looked back.

Rebuilding from 'requires improvement'

As I'm sure you can imagine, staff morale was in the gutter following the inspection. Everyone was fed up, but we also knew we had to address the improvement areas quickly. There were some positives, and we needed to take what we had and work on improving it. But it was hard going – as I'm sure you know, no one really wants to work in an RI school. The parents and community had lost faith in us. It was a hard cross to bear.

At the time, I clearly remember one parent, Mr Copeman, saying to me, 'The thing is, Mrs Savidge, I don't want my son to go into a "requires improvement" school.' I replied, 'Neither do I, Mr Copeman, but we've got to work together to make it better.'

One of the positives from the situation was that our governors were on board and very supportive of what we were doing. Of course, after getting the RI report we were scrutinised to the nth degree. We had a very stringent school improvement plan and had to attend six-weekly meetings with the local authority to make sure we were on track. If you've ever been in that position yourself, you'll know how going to those meetings feels like a walk of shame.

By this time, I had become the substantive headteacher and I wanted to do everything I could to turn our school around. We knew we needed to make significant changes, but there were also areas where we needed to hold our nerve to deliver the best education for our children and our community.

Every year we set a mantra for our school, and in 2014 that mantra was: 'Every child matters, every minute counts.' At this point we had completely restructured the leadership team, and I knew the only way we'd succeed was if I could get everyone on board and working in harmony to reignite our own and the parents' belief in the school.

One of the ways in which I worked to get everyone on board was to meet with the parents. Most days they were cross, and I was fighting fires. To help improve our relationship with the parents, we started a parent council that is run by one of my governors.

> When I first took over as head, I noticed there was a plant outside my new office. It looked bedraggled and wilted – it clearly hadn't been watered for a long time and wasn't doing well. I very nearly walked past it, but then I stopped. Who else would water it if I didn't?
>
> I started watering it, and gradually the plant recovered. This plant became my daily reminder that every part of the school required nurturing, and I couldn't expect my team to do anything I wasn't prepared to do myself.

As funny as it probably sounds, the analogy of watering the plant became really important to me. I needed everyone to do their own equivalent of watering the plant – it was part of the shift in culture that we needed to create, so that ours was a school where everyone would take responsibility.

In May 2014, our HMI (Her Majesty's Inspector then, now His Majesty's Inspector) returned. One sentence in their report stood out, and laid the foundations of everything that was to come:

> Senior leaders and governors are taking effective action to tackle the areas requiring improvement identified in the recent Section 5 inspection.

That visit in May was the last time I saw our HMI. It felt like we had turned a corner, but any elation I felt at having made gains didn't last too long.

Change is hard

For all of us, 2014 had been a tough year. Although staffing was more stable, it was hard to recruit. People didn't want to work in school with so much pressure to improve.

This was when one of my most experienced teachers told me they were leaving because they couldn't do what I was asking of them. I was crushed. I knew I needed to take a step back when I heard this from a great teacher who I trusted deeply. I knew I was wrong, but I didn't know what to do instead. I felt so stuck that I just sat and cried. Not knowing what else to do, I went out and bought cakes. That evening, I scrapped the planned staff meeting and instead we talked about what we could change.

Through this discussion, we stripped a lot of things out. I realised that we had reached the tipping point at which we needed to show more trust in our staff if we were going to continue making progress.

Following the Ofsted review by our local authority, I was told to get rid of three teachers because they weren't good enough. Perhaps you've been put in this situation too. What do you do? I had to decide whether I should manage their departure or work with them. After all, who would replace them if they left? I chose to work with them, and although two of them left, one has remained and became part of the middle leadership team.

As difficult as this period was, our outcomes improved and our leadership team became stable. We could see the strategies we were following were starting to pay off. Clarity had become part of our school culture, and we had a very clear learning and teaching strategy to build on – this continues to this day.

As I've explained, our demographics are diverse, and we felt we needed to develop our own curriculum to do what was right for our children – as if things weren't hard enough already! But the road to 'outstanding' is never about taking the easy option, as I'm sure you're aware. By February 2016, we were ready for our next Ofsted inspection. The call didn't come. By May 2016, we were impatient for our next inspection. To some of you reading this, that might sound strange, but we were ready, and we wanted to show how far we'd come from our RI rating.

The school felt like a pressure cooker that was ready to pop. When the call came, it almost felt like a relief. We had learned so much as a school and we were proud of what we'd achieved.

Zero to hero, and back to zero

During the Ofsted inspection in 2016 I fought for what was right for our school. Unlike in February 2014, we were prepared. At the end of those two days, I was told Clockhouse would be rated 'good'. We were elated, but compared to our previous inspection the improvement areas weren't massive. There was still a nervous two-month wait for the report to be officially published, but when it finally landed on 4 July 2016, everything felt great.

Clockhouse Primary School
Clockhouse Lane, Collier Row, Romford, Essex RM5 3QR

Inspection dates	17–18 May 2016
Overall effectiveness	**Good**
Effectiveness of leadership and management	Good
Quality of teaching, learning and assessment	Good
Personal development, behaviour and welfare	Good
Outcomes for pupils	Good
Early years provision	Good
Overall effectiveness at previous inspection	Requires improvement

Our elation lasted just one day. On 5 July 2016, the SATs results came out... 42% combined. All of a sudden, we found ourselves back at the bottom of that mountain. We knew our plans would need to change again.

Breaking the cycle

Date of inspection	Ofsted grading
Amalgamation (2007)	Infants – Good, Juniors – Satisfactory
February 2009	Satisfactory
November 2011	Good
February 2014	Requires improvement
May 2016	Good
2020	???

As you can see, we had bounced from 'good' to 'satisfactory/requires improvement', then back to 'good', and then to 'requires improvement'. When we achieved our 'good' rating in 2016, we knew we didn't want to repeat that cycle of sliding backwards.

This was when we started talking about how every person on the team was a leader in their own area, whether that was myself as the head, the teachers, the classroom support staff, the office staff or the caretaker. Taking charge in our own areas also meant we needed to be prepared to be wrong sometimes, otherwise we'd never change in the way our children needed us to.

You'll know as well as anyone that being wrong can feel scary. But we found that flipping our perspective around being wrong and taking risks was really helpful. We realised that we needed to take risks and show our children that it is okay to fail. After all, the most successful people in the world take risks, particularly those in the private sector. As Bill Gates famously said, 'To win big, you sometimes have to take big risks.'

Focusing on taking risks was part of the cultural shift we made at Clockhouse. I and the rest of the leadership team started having conversations with all of the staff about the risks that we needed to take this year, and what risks they were going to take themselves in the next year.

These didn't have to be big risks. In fact, we decided starting small was better. We wanted to follow the example set by David Brailsford, the coach for British Cycling, who focused on making marginal gains within the team. We all agreed we'd focus on taking little steps to improve, trying to get 1% better each time.

This was when we really started to hone our school culture. We had already started changing our culture, but now we were ready to do more. This was when I started talking to Sonia at Head's Up about the next stage of our journey – it fit perfectly with our 2017/18 mantra: 'Going above and beyond'.

Understanding school culture

The importance of developing a positive school culture cannot be overstated. We can't escape the fact that if our goal is to provide the best possible learning and work environment, and the best possible education experience, our schools need an identity. Without it, people may end up pulling in different directions and creating disruption rather than working towards the same common goal.

A strong culture provides that sense of identity and a clear common goal. I've learned that whatever improvement our school is working towards, achieving it always requires us to go back to the culture and what is being created in the school. A clear culture not only creates momentum behind improvement, but it also allows that momentum to be directed in whichever way is desired. If you feel as though people in your team are pulling in different directions, this could be a sign that you and your team will benefit from revisiting your school culture and gaining clarity over what it means for all of you.

What exactly is school culture?

Let's go back to basics for a moment. Forgive me if you already have a good grasp of what a school culture is, but I feel it's important that I share my understanding of the concept so we're all on the same page.

For me, a school culture is when *everyone* in the school understands what the school is about, what the school is striving for and what part they play in creating the culture. When I say everyone, I mean everyone, from myself as the headteacher, the senior leadership team, the teaching staff and class-based support staff, the office staff, governors and, of course, the children and parents. We all want consistency in how we act and what we want to achieve. But within that, we want to allow our staff to have their own identity that feeds into the culture we're trying to create.

However, it's worth acknowledging that this culture you're creating is not going to be for everyone. Ensuring your school progresses and develops in the way you want it to requires you to have the right people on board – you want people who *want* to be a part of your culture. I mentioned earlier that two members of staff left when we started making changes at the school in 2014. I'm sure that's a situation most of us have been in as heads. When this happens, we have to remind ourselves that, in the long term, this will be a good thing for our school – though I know sometimes this is easier said than done!

A strong positive culture allows us to define our school and allows people to identify what they want from being part of the school. In terms of recruitment, this allows us to recruit the best possible people – namely those who want to be part of the school and our culture. What I'll share in the rest of this chapter is how we created a culture everyone could understand and fully get behind at Clockhouse Primary.

Creating the cultural shift

Four years after I'd stepped into the head's role, we'd made great progress. Now our focus – our mantra – was on 'making the impossible possible'. However, it turned out there was more to do in relation to our school's culture than I and my senior leadership team had realised.

We thought we had complete buy-in to our school culture, but we hadn't. When I asked the staff to articulate the school's vision and values, they couldn't. It wasn't just the staff; the same was true of our parents and children. When we revisited the vision and values, it was easy to see why – it was full of educational jargon that didn't resonate with anyone. Perhaps this is a scenario you can also relate to? It's easily done, and it was a trap we fell into.

We quickly realised we needed clarity on what it means to be a teacher or a member of the class-based support staff at our school. This could unlock 'outstanding' for us, because when everyone is clear about the school's vision and values they know what they need to do, how they need to work and what they need to develop. They can lead their own professional development and understand the importance of buying into the vision and values, thereby helping to develop the culture.

Achieving clarity within the team is a great way to assess your school's vision and values. Does everyone seem to know what they need to do, how they need to work and what they need to develop? If, like us, the answer is, 'Not exactly', this is a great cue to revisit your vision.

We didn't just revisit our vision; we developed our 'cultural ecosystem'. This is a combination of:

- **Our vision** – why we do what we do.
- **Our values** – what behaviour we value most on this journey.
- **Our strategic priorities** – what is most important to us as a school.

When we examined our current cultural ecosystem, we realised that while we had all of these components in place they weren't clear enough, they didn't resonate and not everyone was fully onboard and clear about our priorities and expectations. Our vision was full of buzzwords that no one really remembered. It ticked the boxes, but it didn't really *mean* a great deal. Logically it made sense, but we didn't feel it in our hearts and souls. I'm sure this is something you've experienced in at least one school you've worked in.

With Sonia's guidance, we decided to work on our values and strategic priorities first. Why? Because these two elements underpin the vision. Having approached writing our vision in this way, all I can tell you is that it works! How it looks will be different for your school, but if writing a vision is something that's been challenging, you are likely to benefit from this new perspective, just as we did.

Our vision was born: 'Our school, a family and a home for everyone.'

> We are not just a school, we are home!
>
> We lay the foundations for each individual's future and for dreams to be fulfilled – whatever they may be.
>
> No two bricks are the same but are accepted for their uniqueness and are placed in their own special way to meet their needs.
>
> The cement bonds us together as a family to keep us strong, stable and safe.
>
> We are all safe and happy under one roof, we are protected from the elements and prepared to weather every storm.
>
> The key to success unlocks the door to future achievements unseen before.
>
> The windows show us the reflections of our future self as ready, respectful and responsible adults.
>
> Collaboratively, together our home is decorated with challenge and the rooms are furnished with fun.
>
> All around, a variety of trees grow naturally from the seed of success. With nurture and care anything is possible.
>
> So we are not just a school, we are a home that provides a champion for all as well as timeless experiences and skills for a brighter future.
>
> And that is why we are called Clockhouse.
>
> Ring the bell, we're always here!

As you can see, our vision isn't the average vision you might expect for a school. It focuses on the analogy of a house. When the senior leadership team launched the vision in 2019, we received a round of applause when we finished reading it. When I looked around the room, I could see that everyone was really on board. Some of them welled up with tears as they listened. Our vision resonates with us – staff, children, parents, in fact our whole community. Each head's challenge is to find a vision that resonates with their community – this does!

Because of this resonance, we achieved great buy-in when we launched it, and during the Covid-19 pandemic it really helped pull everyone together. Our vision underpins all the decisions we make and has become a collective responsibility for our community.

Among the 100 staff, all but two were on board immediately. One left the school shortly after we launched our vision. The other reflected, realised it was for her and remains a pivotal member of our team today. Having that vision empowered them to make a very conscious choice about whether they were up for the journey ahead. We also had to accept that if it wasn't for them, that was okay and they could leave with love.

Now, any member of our community can tell you what our vision is and what our values are. They understand the cultural ecosystem that underpins everything we do. This was instrumental in our development as a school that delivers an outstanding education for our children.

Values

To create our vision, we had to really unpick our values. Again, this was hard work. It was not enough to decide what values we believed in, which was difficult enough. We had to create deep resonance and clarity about what they would mean in practice, in a way that everyone would remember and recognise. Our values, along with our vision, underpin everything we do.

Values are a useful tool. For example, as a senior leadership team, we know that if something upsets us it's often because it's jarring with one of our values. We've found that this is a really useful way to frame discussions. Paul and Ian will discuss values in much greater detail in chapters 4 and 8 respectively.

Of course, all three components of our cultural ecosystem feed back into our school improvement plan and our work as a whole.

Better than good

In January 2020 the phone rang, and we went into a Section 8 inspection.

We wanted an 'outstanding' rating, not only because of all the work we'd put in but because we felt we owed it to the community. I owed it to Mr Copeman, who didn't want his child to go to an RI school (incidentally, his fourth child is now at Clockhouse!). I felt I owed it to the staff for all the hard work they put in.

It was an intense two days. During my first inspection as head in 2014, my staff told me they were all behind me. I was leading from the front. This time it was different though. We were alongside one another, in it together, ready to fight to the bitter end. To me, it was the perfect demonstration of how far our culture had come.

When the inspection ended, everyone was desperate to know whether we'd broken the cycle of going backwards from 'good'. We had. Our report said:

> Clockhouse Primary School continues to be a 'good' school. There is enough evidence of improved performance to suggest that the school could be judged 'outstanding' if we were to carry out a Section 5 inspection now.

One thing the inspector said stood out for me above all else: 'There's a clear spirit and vision that grabs hold of you as soon as you come into the building.' That didn't make it into the report, but I wish it had, because to me, that says everything there is to say about our culture.

Outstanding in all areas

Following the 2020 inspection, we knew Ofsted would be heading back our way sooner than usual. Now let's be clear, it's not all about Ofsted. Our drive has always been to provide the best possible educational experience for our children, and Ofsted simply provides us with an external validation of this. Our report was published in February 2020, and we all know what happened in March 2020. The pandemic meant we ended up waiting three years and five months for the graded inspection, with that call coming in June 2023. Now was our time to shine – in one way it was probably the easiest inspection of the five I had during my first 10 years of headship (we were so ready), but in another way it was the hardest.

Ofsted sent a big inspection team, and the stakes were high. It was a gruelling two days, but our whole community shone. Everyone was on message, and every single person, without fail, did their bit to show those inspectors how far our school had come. We had worked so hard and now was our time.

The irony was not lost on me or the lead inspector when, during the final keeping-in-touch meeting at lunchtime on the second day, she said to me, 'I need to ask you about something – I have not seen any food technology.' As she got to the end of the word 'technology', there was a knock at my door and after being invited in, the Cookery Club walked in with couscous and fruit kebabs. The lead just looked at me and said, 'Well, you could not have planned that!', then shut her laptop and that was the end of the conversation about food technology. But it wasn't about food technology per se, it just showed how far our school had come.

Nine years and nine months from watering that plant and taking on that broken school, and five inspections later, Clockhouse Primary was graded 'outstanding in all areas'. What a journey, what an achievement for our community. Are we perfect? No. Is there always more to do? Of course. But our drive to provide the best possible learning experience for our children had been externally validated.

The power of culture

A strong culture is undeniably powerful, but sometimes it can be hard to quantify the impact it has. The following are examples of the positive impacts of our school culture.

The impact on outcomes

There is a direct link between school culture and outcomes, the strength of which depends on what we mean by 'outcomes'. There is naturally a link between culture and end-of-key-stage outcomes. This is data driven (based on end of key stage 2 SATs results). However, there is a far greater link between outcomes and culture when you consider it in terms of behaviour, attitudes and the wellbeing of children, staff, parents and the community.

When we are clear and understand what we are about through having a well-structured cultural ecosystem, it allows us to focus on everything else because we know what is expected of us and how to act and behave, and it enables us to provide a happy and harmonious school where we can focus on learning. We can put the children we teach at the centre of what we do and give them the best possible chance for future success, whatever that may look like for each individual. The 'outstanding' judgement we received from Ofsted in 2023 is a response to our commitment to providing the best possible education every day.

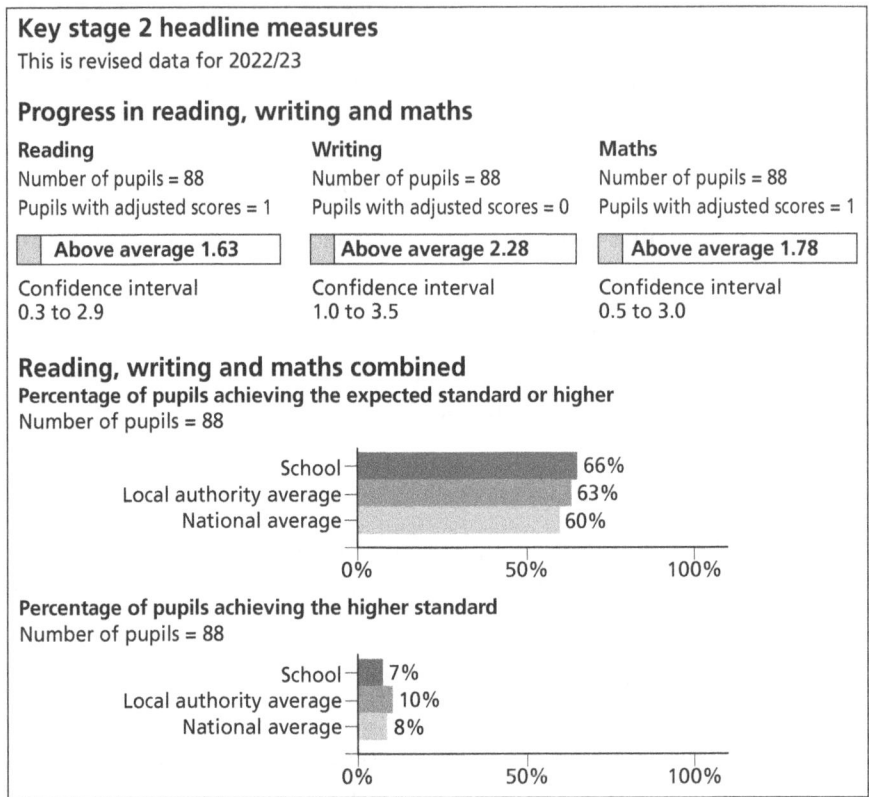

The impact on performance management

To deliver that outstanding level of education, everyone on our team needs to be continuously working on their own professional development.

We need to hold people accountable when they are not meeting expectations, but also celebrate when they are. When working at their best, people will lead their own development. They will recognise the challenges and work hard to overcome them, leading to a better school for everyone, particularly the children.

When I became the head of Clockhouse, I inherited a performance management system that was very formulaic, but it worked. However, one day I was challenged (yes, by Sonia again) in my thinking and this led to a complete renovation of the process. If you're using a standard performance management system, you may want to explore alternatives like we did – as I said, what we had worked, but what we now use delivers real transformation. Our cultural ecosystem is what makes our new performance management process possible, because this has given all of us a common way in which to talk about behaviour as well as performance.

Our performance management process is written by the person it belongs to, not by senior leaders. We have development conversations. This allows us to work with staff to develop them and in turn develop the school. We introduced instructional coaching to develop each individual. The senior leadership team now has catch-ups with individual staff members every half term when we work on their development together. This allows us to have an open discussion about where each person is, where they want to be and how to get there.

Currently this works very well for our teaching staff. Recently we've developed this further by considering our culture in terms of how this links to staff wellbeing and workload. Our aim is to make staff more responsible for their wellbeing so they can give their very best every day to our children as well as looking after themselves.

The teaching staff are very positive about having these regular catch-ups with senior leaders. This has allowed our school to develop at a faster rate, as individual teachers are all working to develop themselves, which collectively develops the school. All of this contributes to delivering an outstanding educational environment.

We could have just continued with the box-ticking performance management approach that we had, but being brave and acknowledging that what we were doing was not nearly as good as it could be was a necessary first step for us. As with everything, people will not follow if they don't know where they are going, so before taking this step with the staff, as leaders we had to be clear on what we wanted it to look like, what we wanted to get out of it, the rationale for change and the impact it would have on our culture. If you're thinking of making such a change,

I urge you to consider these questions before doing anything and ensure clarity in your approach to make it as successful as possible.

The impact on recruitment

A clear culture creates a clear identity. Once a school culture is established and embedded, although it is ever evolving it becomes easier to bring new people in. These new recruits then know what you're all about, and they want to be part of that. This allows both you and them to quickly identify whether they are the right fit for your team.

Sometimes, even if someone knows what you're about, once they become part of your culture they realise it's not for them. We recently found ourselves in this very situation – a new member of staff found our expectations hard to meet. They therefore took the decision, without any prompting from any of our senior leaders, to leave the school.

While this was sad, no school can be a good fit for everybody. Having a strong cultural ecosystem quickly ensured this person's wellbeing was maintained, and they made the decision that was right for them and the school. Working in an environment with a culture and values you haven't bought into is not sustainable in the long term.

That said, we also have many people who want to come and work at our school *because* they buy into our culture. In fact, we have more people wanting to join our school than we have roles for, and given the current recruitment challenges this is something I'm really grateful for. Something we regularly hear at interviews is that they understand the vision and our values, and they want to be part of our family.

Challenges in creating a positive school culture

As senior leaders establishing a school culture, there are several challenges that we need to overcome before the real work begins. There are three areas that I believe are particularly critical – and that we had to focus on in our journey at Clockhouse.

'Copying' school culture

The first challenge is the mistaken belief that you can 'copy' a successful culture from another school. School culture is personal to the school you are working in and to the leaders at that school. You cannot transfer someone else's ready-made culture to your setting; sadly, it simply doesn't work like that.

You have to be pragmatic when thinking about and understanding school culture. As school leaders, we'll each have our own ideal culture and vision for the school, but these alone do not provide an overnight fix. The truth is, it will take time and hard work to get your cultural ecosystem in place, and then constant work to embed it.

My advice is to begin by examining the unique context of your school. Dive deep into where your school is and use that understanding to build the culture and vision your school needs. This may involve asking yourself some difficult questions. I found these questions particularly useful when I did this exercise at our school:

- Is your ideal culture and vision what your children and your school need?
- Is it relevant to the school context?
- Is it relevant to the place your school is currently in?

Setting the culture

The second challenge comes in the form of accepting that not everyone should be involved in setting the school culture. I used to believe everyone should have a say in the process, but my view was challenged when we created our school culture at Clockhouse Primary. With external support, the senior leadership team worked on setting the culture and vision for the school, and then communicated it clearly to the staff to ensure that everyone would buy in.

Communicating the culture

This brings us to the third challenge to creating a positive culture: a lack of clarity, which results in poor communication of the culture and vision. Clarity is essential, because if we, as senior leaders, are unclear on the culture we want our school to have and how we are going to create it, we won't be able to communicate it to the rest of the community.

Poor communication risks creating division, as people from across the school body will not understand the school's goals and future developments, why they are being asked to do certain things or how the school is going to improve. By contrast, when we have clarity over our culture, vision and values, it's much easier to see how to embed it into every part of the school community.

In my experience, if culture stands alone, rather than permeating everything, it becomes another tick-box exercise. When it is embedded into everything, every task has a clear purpose that moves the school in the right direction.

So, how do we embed our culture into every aspect of life at our school? As hard as it sounds, we first have to accept that this work will never end. Communicating culture is not something that happens once and then it's done.

I've found the key is to communicate your culture in multiple ways, over and over again. When you can do this well, those around you will start to see the impact of your culture. They'll have a clear understanding of your identity and what you want to develop. And when they start to see the positive change in direction, they will buy in and become advocates for your culture.

What does your school's culture look like?

You can see the culture of a school living everywhere, regardless of how intentionally you have created it. Take a moment to think about the schools you've worked in or visited. How would you identify their cultures? It probably takes less time than you think to get a sense of a school's culture.

With that in mind, how do you think people from outside your school community would describe your culture after visiting you? First impressions really do count. Perception is very important in a school setting and shapes the school environment.

The topic of perception in schools is often debated. Some may say it doesn't much matter in the grand scheme of things; others may argue that first impressions are the most important. What I've come to realise is that a first impression of a school should, ideally, give a sense of the school's vision and values. Making our school identity clear to everyone creates unity and allows everyone to drive towards the same key messages.

If, as leaders, we've decided something is important in the context of our vision and values, it's important that this is maintained at every level. If we have rules to support our vision, values and culture, they need to be upheld. After all, what's the point in having a rule if you're not going to uphold it? This goes beyond first impressions and stretches into how everyone who spends time at your school, whether a pupil, teacher, other member of staff, parent or visitor, perceives the environment.

As school leaders, we need to understand and manage perception in our schools. If we don't, we're in danger of having an environment that is not orderly, where everybody has different expectations. This can lead to fractures in our school culture.

Being clear about our own expectations is not enough, as I'm sure you know. We need to communicate our expectations clearly, and model them in everything we do. If we are not modelling the behaviours we want to see, we cannot expect other people to demonstrate them either. If we are not communicating clearly, we cannot expect others to know what we are thinking.

When we think about this from a distance, it seems obvious, but it is easy to forget the importance of daily communication around values and expectations in the busyness of the school day. I know that's a trap I've fallen into in the past. Communicating our expectations is only one half of the puzzle though. We also have to ensure we hold people to account in the right way when certain behaviours are not happening or when our values are not being displayed.

In our school, we work hard to ensure we uphold our values. We work to the principle that the attitude or the behaviour you walk past is the attitude or behaviour you are willing to accept – think back to my unwatered pot plant. You need to know what is and is not acceptable.

For example, two of our key school values are excellence and respect, along with ensuring we care for our environment. One of the important ways we live this is by providing a tidy, well-presented environment. You could argue a tidy environment doesn't necessarily make learning and teaching better, but it's about perception. Our school context means that some of our pupils don't experience a tidy, well-presented environment at home, and we want to offer them something different.

In our school, the commitment to our values in everything we do ensures a positive impression starts from the moment we step onto the school grounds. What we see, hear and feel should reflect our culture and uphold our vision and values.

When you finish reading this chapter, I invite you to look around your school. I don't just mean take a cursory glance; I mean really *look*. It's easy to think you see everything because you're there every day. But do you really look at it?

Use the following prompts to help you see more:

- Look up.
- Look down.
- Look left.
- Look right.
- Look at your school from the children's eye level.

It's eye-opening when you look in every corner, in every cupboard, to see what others see. What does it say to you? Is it good enough? Could it be better?

I also find it useful to ask myself what we want a visitor to think when they leave our school. What do we want them to say about us? We need to ensure, as school leaders in a school community, that we give anyone who visits our school every opportunity to say and think what we want them to, not what we don't.

So, take a moment to have a really good look around your school and make sure those people say, feel, hear and see what you want them to. It may mean asking some hard questions – I know we had to. It may mean changing some things, but it will be for the better and it will enhance your culture. Personally, I find this exercise enlightening and find value in repeating it at regular intervals.

Leaning into cultural evolution

Culture is a process that, like a curriculum, is never 'done' and is always evolving. It has to develop to ensure it stays relevant. At the start you have your key principles that underpin your culture, vision and values, but it's how you use those to align with your school improvement process and your wider school ethos that's key. This will develop over time. Once you have your basis, you can move forward and deepen that culture, regularly revisiting it to ensure it is embedded into and drives everything you do.

On our bumpy journey, I learned that culture needs to run through every aspect of school improvement, to be present in every part of your day and be modelled by those around you. If you are doing something that doesn't link back to your values and vision – and therefore your culture – it's impossible to move the school in the direction you want.

Some of our children come from very vulnerable backgrounds. We aim to provide them with the best possible education experience, whether that be academic, social or emotional. Our values and vision drive what we want to do, why we want to do it and what we want to give to our children. One of our values is excellence, which we strive to provide for our children, and everything we do is to give them the best possible chance of success.

The long and bumpy road to 'outstanding'

When I became the head of Clockhouse Primary School, we would describe ourselves as 'the broken school', and we historically had outcomes that were below national standards. We've done a lot since then! One of the most pivotal changes was developing our culture, linking this to everything we do and driving our school improvement. Now we sit in line with or above national averages and our progress scores are high.

As you've read, it's taken 10 years, incredible determination, hard work, many happy times, and some very sad times to get where we are today:

a school that provides the very best for a community in challenging circumstances. Not only have the hard, objective outcomes in terms of data improved, but so too have the 'softer' outcomes – our children and parents are happy, as are our staff. Staff wellbeing is considered in a way that impacts positively on the provision we give our children.

The impact of culture on our pupils in terms of outcomes, whether they be 'hard' or 'soft', is clear. Seeing the children from our SEND unit being embraced and loved by everyone in our school shows me we have created a culture of real inclusion.

Our culture is used to hold all our children to account in the way they act, and it underpins our behaviours and our expectations of everything we do. All the members of our community, whether in the immediate or wider community, are expected to live up to the same standards.

Every member of staff knows what's expected of them. We have clearly defined key performance indicators that are broken down and linked clearly to the role that person plays within the school and the whole cultural ecosystem. Our values are broken down in terms of our behaviours and what these look like at different levels. This allows everyone to understand their part in making Clockhouse the place it is each and every day. It ensures everyone knows what's expected of them, whatever their role.

This approach makes positive conversations easy, as you can easily find things to praise people for. It also makes difficult conversations a lot easier because they're based on what is expected and the behaviours we want to see. It allows people to identify their gaps and what they need to do to progress, and to make plans to better themselves, which in turn will better the school.

One of the fundamental elements underpinning a strong school culture is a clear vision. If you want to start working on your school's culture, here are my top tips to help keep you on track.

TOP TIPS

- ★ Be clear about what you want to create before you do anything else. The sooner you get this right, the easier it will be to really, deeply improve your school.
- ★ Develop your cultural ecosystem and share and promote it widely with your community. This provides the backbone to everything you do, underpinning and driving your development.
- ★ Work tirelessly to develop, tweak, refine and elevate your culture until it is embedded into every aspect of your school improvement, development and life. When everything is linked back to your culture, vision and values, it develops a better school for everyone.

Chapter 3:
No-excuses culture – Helen Nicholson

Meet Helen...

Helen Nicholson is the executive headteacher at Stanton Junior School in Milton Keynes. She first joined the school in 1995, teaching there until 2004. However, in 2007 she returned as headteacher. It was a challenging time – the school was in the bottom 100 schools in England and Wales. By 2012, Helen and her team had transformed it into the fourth most improved school in England and Wales. In 2016, they received their first 'outstanding' rating from Ofsted, and this was reaffirmed in 2021. Helen attributes the school's success, in part, to a laser focus on creating a no-excuses culture.

About Stanton Junior School

	School	National average
Pupils with a SEND Education, Health and Care Plan	1.3%	2.5%
Pupils with SEND support	11.9%	13.5%
Pupils whose first language is not English	29.3%	22.0%
Pupils eligible for free school meals at any time during the past six years	41.8%	25.9%

> I completed my third-year teaching practice at Stanton School in the early 1990s. When I arrived on my first day, a Year 5 teacher called Claire welcomed me. She walked me along the corridors and upstairs to the Year 5 and Year 6 area. As we walked in, she smiled at me and said, 'Welcome to your new home!'
>
> Little did I – or she – realise then how meaningful those words were. I think it's fair to say I see Stanton as my home now, and I like to think that the staff and pupils see it as a home for them too.
>
> But making it a happy home, that we can all be proud of, has been a long and winding journey. In this chapter I'll share how we've transformed Stanton from being in the bottom 100 schools in England and Wales to one that has (to date) received two 'outstanding' ratings from Ofsted back-to-back.
>
> My hope is that you'll find one or two golden nuggets in our experiences that you can implement in your own schools on your own journey to 'outstanding'. Personally, I believe our success comes down to our consistency and our no-excuses culture.

Facing up to the challenge

There are many challenges in the world of teaching. Two days are never the same. I took up teaching because I wanted to make a difference, and I wanted children to be successful. To achieve that, I've realised from experience, you need to have a school that has high expectations and wants the best for all pupils. Building a culture that facilitates educational excellence takes time, energy and determination.

As we all know, it is hard work some days, but the rewards you get outweigh the amount of work that you put in. Seeing a happy, positive school where children and teachers alike are working hard and being successful is the biggest reward you can have. And being in an environment that is the opposite of that can therefore feel incredibly demoralising.

My biggest challenge came at the beginning of my headship journey. As a new headteacher at Stanton, I walked into a school that was tired and cluttered. Behaviour wasn't great. Attendance wasn't wonderful. There was very little budget, and I had very few resources to work with. Much of the equipment we did have was broken or damaged. Staff morale was at rock bottom, and many were leaving. The standards for reading, writing and maths were very low. Our combined results when I joined were 42%. Of around 80 primary schools in Milton Keynes, we were always rated within the bottom three.

I looked around me and could see that we needed to do a lot of work. The children that attended this school deserved better, and I was determined to change this for them. That said, this was my first headship, and with hindsight I was taking on a lot more than I realised. I now believe that to be a good thing – if I'd known the full scale of the challenges I faced when I started in 2007, I may well have declined the job!

Where we started

You can see our pupil demographics at the start of this chapter, but to understand where we were, and therefore how far we've come, I'd like to share a bit more about Stanton's history and location. We're a three-form entry school in an area of Bradville, which was one of the original estates in Milton Keynes.

Bradville was originally meant to be temporary housing for the workers building Milton Keynes, yet over 50 years on, these houses, and the community, are still there. The properties in this area of Milton Keynes include a high percentage of social housing. It's considered one of the bottom three most deprived estates in the city. We serve a very interesting catchment area, with high mobility as people move in and out of the estates. We've had Afghan refugee children join us, as well as children from Hong Kong. Our pupil population is very mixed.

In 2008, we were rated satisfactory by Ofsted. Given our location, the community we serve and the challenges we face, it would have been very easy to make excuses for this rating. But I knew that passing the buck wouldn't lead to the improvement our children desperately needed to see. This was when I introduced the concept of a no-excuses culture.

As that culture became firmly embedded in our school, we took big strides forward. By 2012, we had been named the fourth most improved school in England and Wales. In 2013 we won the Southeast Regional Award for the way we used our Pupil Premium funding to close the gap between the children deemed disadvantaged and the rest of the school population. In 2016 we were rated 'outstanding' by Ofsted for the first time.

In my first year at the school, I promised myself that I would take Stanton from 'good' to 'outstanding' – even though at that point we hadn't even got to 'good'. I was determined to put in the hard work, and I truly believed that we could get there. I also knew I'd need everyone to be on board on this journey. What I'll share with you now is how I and the rest of the team have taken Stanton on that journey.

Starting with the staff

As you will be well aware, if your team isn't on board with an initiative or proposed change, it won't get off the ground. When you join a new school, you inherit staff who have been there for a number of years and are used to doing things in their own way, because that's what they've always done. In our situation, what had always been done clearly wasn't enough.

At the start of my headship, I had to find a way to get everyone on board with my vision for what Stanton could become: an outstanding school. I knew the role of a headteacher is to make a difference and further develop the education being delivered in our schools. That's the same whether our school is rated 'outstanding' or 'requires improvement'.

About half the staff were new and fully committed to that journey. However, only half of the teaching staff had been at the school since before my arrival in 2007. Not all were ready to embrace change. As a new head, I came in with a staff training plan and shared it openly. At staff meetings everybody would nod and agree, make notes and show their commitment to whatever I was focusing on. But the reality was very different.

As I walked around the classrooms, I saw some of the teachers were not employing any of the suggestions and were doing their own thing. For example, I can remember one staff meeting where we discussed the value of direct teaching during the main activity. As a staff, we agreed to implement this. However, during learning walks it was evident that although this had been agreed, a few teachers were not direct teaching and instead chose to walk around the room or were sitting at their desks. The opportunity for children to make accelerated progress was therefore being missed.

Some of these teachers believed they were doing the very best they could for the children. The challenge for me was to change their mindset.

This may sound familiar to you. It's tricky to bring everyone on board. I wanted the staff to be moving together as a team, but some of them would put up barriers and use excuses, such as 'the children are low ability' or 'they don't come from a great area'. A 'these kids can't…' narrative was pervasive. It's understandable how any of us can fall into the trap of using excuses for children from challenging backgrounds not performing as expected, but I firmly believed our children could achieve more if we gave them the support and resources they needed.

This belief laid the foundations for our cultural shift. I truly believe that this excuse culture needs to be turned on its head within education. Is the glass half empty or half full? I've always believed in being positive and recognising there are no barriers to learning. There are challenges of course, but they can be, and have been, overcome to enable children to succeed. Stories like ours and the others featured in this book show that it's possible.

What do I mean by a no-excuses culture?

In the simplest terms, a no-excuses culture means that everyone does what we have agreed. No exceptions. This culture is built on the following values:

- There is no excuse for not following agreed procedures and behaviours.
- There is no excuse for not offering ideas and possible solutions to problems.
- There is no excuse for not helping your peers and being part of a supportive community.

- There is no excuse for not believing that together we can achieve anything.

'No excuses' means we all pull together in the same direction. Our no-excuses culture extends far beyond our teaching and leadership team. It has become part of the fabric of our school and is embraced by pupils and parents as well.

The good news is that once the no-excuses culture is in place, it becomes easier to maintain due to a pattern of consistency. Planning lessons becomes easier, whether maths, music or computing. Thanks to our consistent structure and expectations, we all know the pattern regardless of the subject. We don't have excuses for not doing lesson planning. Our expectation is that we learn how to if we don't already know, rather than giving excuses for not doing it.

Having a no-excuses mindset is liberating. It enables teachers to believe every child can do well. Once this culture is embedded it becomes an accepted truth, but embedding it is hard. Sometimes the staff can't, or won't, participate in the concept. Some just need more support in making a change. However, others may decide they would prefer a fresh challenge and working in a different school. It took me a little while to learn this lesson, but once I realised staff moving on was the best outcome and led to a stronger team emerging, I found a new drive for this journey.

I've found it helpful to keep the following two questions at the front of my mind:

1. Why am I doing this role?
2. What is best for these children? (With everything we have to deal with, unfortunately it can be easy to lose sight of this.)

In the spirit of our no-excuses culture, I knew I couldn't point to a lack of experience on my part as a reason for us not making progress, so I signed up for a course on taking your school from 'good' to 'outstanding'. I knew we could achieve more, and it's this positive outlook that helps the school grow from strength to strength.

Where can the no-excuses mindset take you?

In the early 1980s, four men from Jamaica, despite their tropical background, decided to take up a winter sport to represent their nation – the bobsleigh.

They had little experience, and it was an unlikely competition for them to enter. However, they did everything they could, worked as a team, persevered and took on challenges with a positive attitude. (I'm sure you've seen *Cool Runnings*!) Their success was evident when they qualified for the Winter Olympics in 1988, and the Jamaican team won a gold medal at the World Push Championships in Monaco in 2000.

You can see the parallels between the Jamaican bobsled team's approach and a no-excuses culture, particularly in schools serving areas of high deprivation and facing challenges such as high numbers of children with English as a second language. It's easy to say you're not going to succeed because the odds seem stacked against you, but these children deserve the best.

From my experience, hard work, perseverance and teamwork can yield results, not only in reading, writing and maths, but also in other elements of education such as the arts, humanities, sport and STEAM. Despite discouragement from some, having a no-excuses culture and doing the best for the children can lead to success, just like Jamaica found in 2000 after persevering with training for a winter sport in a tropical climate.

Reflection questions

The following questions can be used to help you to start developing a no-excuses mindset in your school and to measure your progress:

- How many ideas and initiatives in your school have 100% of your team delivering them, 100% of the time?
- What is the school's main priority? How many staff are delivering your main priority 100% of the time? What 'reasons' (excuses) do those who are not delivering give for not doing so? How can you overcome these 'reasons' (excuses)?
- What 'narratives' (excuses) exist in your school? Some may be obvious, but others will be harder to spot. They may include 'these kids', 'this area', 'this school', 'this government', 'this funding', 'this

SEND pressure', 'recruitment', etc. (I'm not saying these aren't challenges – they are, but I really believe we can, and have to, overcome them.)
- What beliefs and excuses are holding you back as a leader?
- What are the practices in your classroom or school? Does everyone use them well? If not, why?
- What great methods are being used in your school that are worth embedding deeper into your teaching team's practice?
- Are you allowing the children that you teach to be as successful as they can be?
- If you believe all children can make accelerated progress, how can you enable pupils to make accelerated progress in lessons?

Building our no-excuses culture, one subject at a time

Embedding a no-excuses culture in our school did not happen overnight. But it was essential to achieve my vision to give every child the best education possible, so they are able to realise their full potential and are prepared for their future, regardless of the real or perceived barriers.

To deliver this, I needed a team who had the skills to lead within the school to ensure a no-excuses culture permeated. But it was also important that they felt safe offering their own suggestions and ideas about how to improve the school and education we provided.

I had appointed a lot of new staff, many of whom were young and new to teaching. They had energy, drive and fresh ideas, and were keen to make lessons fun and develop the learning environment. They wanted to share their vision and ideas, and it was important to me that they were empowered to share and felt listened to.

I remember being made to feel the opposite in my first year of being a teacher. I attended a Year 4 and Year 5 meeting to discuss the 3D display for the foyer. I started to offer an idea and was immediately interrupted by the senior teacher, who told me categorically, 'You can't decide anything!' I can still hear their voice now and remember how it made me feel so small and not worthy. I couldn't understand why I hadn't been able to even finish my sentence.

I didn't want any of the staff at my school to be made to feel small and that they could not offer an idea or suggestion, regardless of how long they had been working at the school. This is why I will always encourage and welcome staff to make suggestions, giving them the opportunity to speak in the knowledge they are in a safe place.

I also knew that changing everything in one go would mean nothing got finished and that would be disheartening, so we broke the process down. We identified and developed one area at a time, focusing on doing that one thing really well. This started with looking at the environment, then behaviour policy, and then developing the curriculum one subject at a time.

No excuses for poor behaviour

As you'd expect given our situation when I started, we had to look at behaviour within our school. I quickly realised that although there was a behaviour policy, it wasn't being implemented. So, to all intents and purposes, there was no behaviour policy. You know as well as I do that it doesn't matter how good your teachers are, if the behaviour among your pupils isn't right, and the children aren't learning in their lessons, they're not going to get anywhere.

We needed something simple and memorable, so we introduced our PROUD code of behaviour. This stands for:

- **P**romise to be honest and always tell the truth.
- **R**espect each other and our school.
- **O**pen minded and eager to learn.
- **U**nderstand each other, listen carefully and talk quietly.
- **D**o your best at all times.

I chose this code of conduct quite early on in my time at Stanton because we needed something that everyone could buy into, no matter who they were within our school community. Everyone from our midday supervisors, admin staff and teachers to our senior leadership team, the pupils and the parents could understand our minimum expectations around behaviour with this simple mnemonic.

We displayed it everywhere around the school and included it as part of our PSHE (personal, social, health and economic) lessons to help the children fully understand and live by the five rules. We've also found these rules are especially useful when challenging behaviour because it gives everyone a shared vocabulary. It makes the implementation consistent and ensures everyone is treated fairly. This code of conduct applies to our staff just as much as our pupils, and we all know this. We even chose the song 'Proud' by M People's Heather Small as our school song!

In the years since we've introduced the PROUD code of conduct, we've developed it so that we now give out PROUD points to children who exhibit these behaviours. That's been received very positively.

Our PROUD code of conduct also led to the introduction of restorative practices, which I'm sure many of you reading this have already implemented in your schools. Restorative practice is a method that involves two parties discussing how an action or event had made them feel, to enable them to move forward positively and build and maintain healthy relationships. The PROUD mnemonic supports this practice as it allows our children to start thinking about their own behaviours and talk about them when issues arise.

The pupils found it easier to talk about why they had done something that went against one of those behaviours, and how it made them feel. Whether it was a teacher or member of support staff who had that conversation, we found that giving the children a chance to share their insights and talk through an incident led to much faster improvements in behaviour.

Again, this helped establish a strong no-excuses culture in our school that threads its way through staff and pupils alike. One of my favourite stories to illustrate this is about two boys who were in trouble and had been sent to me to deal with. However, when they arrived at my office, all the support staff were waiting for a quick briefing. I couldn't delay that session, otherwise it would impact everyone in the school. So, I sat the boys outside the staff room (but away from each other on separate chairs a few metres apart) while I gave the briefing.

When I came out after ten minutes, one of them turned to me and said, 'It's alright, miss, we've sorted it out. We've talked about it.' They shook hands with each other, and I sent them back to their classes. Our no-excuses culture and the process of restorative justice had been so deeply instilled in them that they were able to action it themselves.

Consistency of consequences

Taking responsibility to sort out what isn't working no longer falls solely on my shoulders as the head. My team doesn't need any prompting from me to fix any issues they notice.

As an example, one afternoon after school I found most of the teaching staff having a discussion about a consequence chart. They had realised there wasn't always consistency in the consequences faced by children across different year groups and classes for their actions. To avoid one child facing harsher or more lenient consequences than another, the teaching team took ownership and devised a list of what types of actions and behaviour were sometimes seen and what they considered were acceptable consequences. These included five minutes off a break, or not going out for lunch one day.

We've since taken this one step further and now ask the children what they feel the consequences of their actions should be as part of the restorative practices we already had in place. I can assure you that they are much harsher on themselves than we ever are. We often find we have to bring it down a notch. For example, they might tell me that they feel they need to miss ten lunch breaks, when in our view missing one or two would suffice!

Behaviour improved significantly using a consistent approach and clear boundaries. Fixed-term exclusions were being used for a number of children during my first year as head. However, the impact is clear to see, with exclusions now extremely rare. Focusing on positive behaviour supported by a range of whole-school rewards, including PROUD points, value gems, a golden moments book and Stanton star awards, embeds expectations and allows all children to achieve.

Back to basics

By the end of my first year, I felt we'd made a lot of progress on the school environment and behaviour. But those improvements weren't enough if we still had children who were unable to read! We applied the mantra, 'Take one thing and do it really well', to each subject in turn, starting with reading.

Reading

The first issue we identified was a lack of any consistent teaching approach for reading – which impacted all subjects. There was no real love or desire for reading and books within the school. We knew this needed to change. Our research as a senior leadership team led us to phonics, so we invested in a two-day training course for all our staff as well as the resources we needed to roll out the phonics programme. We also had the whole school assessed – we needed to know what we were working with.

If you're planning to do something similar at your school, my first piece of advice is not to rush it. You have to make sure everything is in place before launching a new programme, otherwise it won't work. We started this process towards the end of my first year as head, and by the time we returned in September, we were ready.

We wanted the children to enjoy reading, so we made it a priority for the first hour of the day when the children are at their best, most alert and ready to learn. Assessing the whole school meant we could group children by ability, rather than age, for these sessions. In our first year that meant we had some Year 6 children in with our Year 3 children. Far from causing issues for the children or parents, this led to rapid progress.

To highlight the importance of reading, we displayed it in every classroom. This ensured our work on phonics was fed into other areas of the curriculum. We also regularly changed the reading groups so the children could move through the different bands as quickly as possible.

We knew that a lack of consistency in teaching had been an issue in the past, so we invested in a leader for the phonics and reading programme. Their job was to ensure it was being taught properly, to support staff and team teach and to provide feedback. We put particular emphasis on positive feedback and celebrating what was going well.

Finally, we refurbished our library and got rid of quite a few books – some of which were older than any of the teaching staff – and invested in new reading material. By the end of that year, we could see that our focus had paid off. When we started, 85% of our children needed to be on the phonics programme in the first year. Once the programme was embedded within the first couple of years, we saw this percentage decrease dramatically to around 9%. Many of these children have SEND or have EAL (English as an additional language) and are new to the country.

Our pupils had made phenomenal progress thanks to the hard work and dedication everyone showed. Reading became the key to unlocking all our other subjects.

Maths

After the success of our phonics programme, we turned our attention to maths. Many of the overarching challenges were the same – low levels in Year 6, everyone using their own teaching styles. In other words, a lack of consistency.

We knew the teaching methods needed to be reorganised to make sure all the children were being taught in the same way. We spent time researching to find the most efficient methods for teaching maths – ones that the children could easily understand and that we, as a teaching team, could easily break down. Doing so meant the children learned and developed much quicker.

As with the phonics programme, the whole team attended a two-day training scheme, and we invested in the resources and materials we needed. We also got the whole school assessed. However, when we rolled out the new method of teaching a new maths programme, we didn't intermingle age groups like we had done for reading. This is because, unlike with reading, the use of differentiation and setting across a year group enables teachers to meet the needs of the children and teach the maths curriculum for their year group.

As before, we focused on having maths displays in every class and we made sure there was a leader for the maths programme who could ensure the consistency of the teaching, support everyone, team teach and give feedback on areas of good practice. Once again, this approach worked for us. It's a system we've since repeated many times across multiple subjects.

Foundation subjects

Every curriculum subject now has a clear structure in terms of how it is delivered. PE has become a particular strength at our school, and we offer three hours of physical education a week for every child. Our sports team delivers high-quality lessons with a learning objective, context, skills and knowledge with success criteria, just like in any other subject.

You may be wondering how we are able to allocate three hours a week to PE! This was actually a change that came out of the Covid-19 pandemic. When we returned to normal school life, we reflected on the time spent waiting in the corridor to get the children filed into the hall for face-to-face assemblies, and we realised it could be better utilised by adjusting the timetable and freeing up learning time. This alone freed up three more hours of PE a week. This allows the children to burn off energy, become fit and healthy, and enjoy the variety of activities that we offer them.

The academic subjects can be challenging for some of our children, but PE is something they love and can succeed at more easily. Like all other subjects, it builds on skills, develops the child and, most importantly, benefits their wellbeing. The successes they gain from this has given them confidence in themselves. This feeds into a can-do approach to other subjects as well.

Valuing all the subjects equally has built a positive, successful and consistent learning environment. Both children and staff know what the expectations are and that everyone can have a go and succeed. This enables our teachers to develop themselves and their subject area, and provides the best opportunities we can offer for the children.

Our 'one subject at a time' approach gathered momentum as the teachers adopted the process of what was happening in the core subjects and used it to develop their own subjects. In doing so, they developed themselves and grew into leaders.

As we know, one person alone cannot do everything within a school. With the no-excuses culture now embedded, our teachers know they can share their ideas for change or make suggestions for improvements. Their input adds wealth to the curriculum and a richness of ideas and opportunities for the children.

Going from outstanding to... more outstanding

Once our teachers had reached the level of outstanding, we faced a rather wonderful dilemma: how do you make outstanding teachers even more outstanding? It's a great problem to have, and one tactic that we've found particularly effective is assigning buddy pairs.

Each spring, we buddy up people who would not necessarily work together. Often, they're not in the same year group or even in the same key stage. They watch each other teach, which feeds into our no-excuses culture in several ways. If you know someone is coming to watch you, you do your best. You want to show them that you're consistent in your approach.

This helps our teachers really consider what they are teaching and the structure of their lesson, which is always a good professional development point. It's also useful to see how you observe each other and see different things. You can be reminded of activities, tasks or ways of doing things that you can easily implement into your own teaching. We also take this approach further afield by visiting other schools, both local and further afield.

Peer observations are also a great way to remind everyone of our expectations. When we've had more experienced teachers join our team and go into this buddy system, they often tell us that in other schools even if expectations are communicated clearly, they've never had anyone check to ensure those expectations are being met.

This exercise is about far more than just checking in on each other; it's a valuable learning opportunity. In fact, it's a privilege to be given the chance to watch other people teach – how often do you get to do that? But a byproduct of this process is that accountability around consistency and our culture is embedded.

My favourite thing about this system is the golden nuggets that teachers come out of these lessons with. We ask everyone to make a note of and share at least one thing they are going to take back to their own practice after watching a lesson. Sometimes it's something they've forgotten about; other times it's something brand new. One benefit is that the implementation of these golden nuggets is easy. In fact, I believe the best nuggets are the ones that cost nothing, take seconds to implement, but have the biggest impact.

We also do a lot of review activities as a whole-staff team, rather than restricting this to senior leadership. We've found this approach is inspirational and gives our teachers ideas they can use in their own classrooms – just like the buddy pair system.

For example, when we do a book scrutiny exercise focusing on one subject, it's lovely how the different year teams have been inspired by each other in terms of the types of activities they've introduced to their lessons. It's also fascinating to see how these activities have been adapted to suit different year groups.

In the early days of being a headteacher, book scrutiny exercises were carried out by the senior leadership team and took more of a 'done to' rather than a 'done with' approach. Although we looked at marking and work in books, identifying strengths and areas for a teacher to work on, this activity was done in isolation. It became very time consuming and had minimal value and impact.

We therefore changed our approach and recognised the value of teachers being inspired by colleagues. This activity offered the opportunity for sharing new ideas, starter activities, differentiation, simple but effective ideas for presenting work and marking ideas. It also reminded staff of expectations of marking and presentation for all. Even our younger children can underline neatly, and low-ability children can complete a task to the best of their ability – no excuses. There was a wealth of knowledge to be shared and used.

Now, book scrutiny exercises are a whole-staff activity. We provide a proforma of agreed focus and subjects for the term, and teachers look at each other's books. At the end we always share the written feedback, and the staff enjoy the process. It is far more meaningful and useful, and a teacher will always enjoy it more if one of their ideas is complimented.

Looking at displays is another great way of sharing good practice. You can see how simple ideas make your displays three-dimensional and interactive, whether it be a washing line with some pegs on, where the children can sort things, or sticky notes, where children can respond to an open-ended question.

These sessions, where we collectively look at each other's work, help to keep expectations high. When one year group is able to see how hard other year groups are working, everyone raises their game.

To develop excellence in teaching on a daily basis, we know we need to encourage routines, practices, expectations and the participation of the children, which combine to accelerate progress. This, to me, is what consistently excellent teaching looks like. I'm open about this with my team, because I know it is this drive, culture and ethos that will lead to an exceptional school culture.

Working smarter, not harder

I know some people believe that a no-excuses mindset equates to more work for teachers who already feel they are working hard, but I'd like to challenge this. In my experience, a no-excuses mindset does not mean more work – rather, it's a different way of working, one where everyone works smarter, not harder.

For instance, I once observed a new staff member teaching a lesson and could see they were working extremely hard. They were doing most of the talking, finishing off the children's answers, even reading the text to the children. The children enjoyed the performance, but it didn't necessarily lead to accelerated progress. Perhaps you've seen such a lesson yourself?

While I appreciated the effort this teacher was putting in, it isn't how we like to teach at Stanton. Though it's understandable why this teacher, and many others, work so hard hard – they worry about the children getting things wrong and then fear letting the children speak, especially during observations – but this can be counterproductive. We know identifying areas that may have confused a child provides an opportunity for

55

reteaching and for other children to offer support. Moreover, the child may be further along in their understanding than anticipated, allowing for quicker progress.

However, on the surface it can feel easier to keep teaching the way we always have. After all, it takes time – yours and the teacher's – to develop a practice. As a head, it's easier to accept the reasons (or excuses) about why teachers teach in a particular way than it is to embed a cultural change. But accepting the status quo ultimately doesn't give our children what they need. You're reading this book because you want to do even better for the children and team at your school, and that means you don't shy away from the effort that it takes.

But as I've said, the no-excuses mindset is not about teachers working harder, but about using the best practices we have agreed on to enable children to make the most progress in class. It might feel harder at the start, but when you work smarter, everything ends up feeling easier. The key is using quality-first teaching as well as a consistent, positive approach in lessons that actively involves children in their learning. We put a lot of work into crafting each subject so children achieve accelerated learning, and 'no excuses' means we all need to learn to use this well, and then improve from there.

> **Looking for continuous improvement**
>
> Naturally, during Covid-19, our teachers were using PowerPoints with voice overs to deliver their lessons. As you may expect (and have experienced in your school), these presentations had become longer than they would have been if delivered in person. However, when we returned to the classroom after Covid-19, the presentations didn't shrink – they only seemed to grow!
>
> Many of the teachers had far too many slides and producing them was taking too much time. We could see that the workload balance was tipping in the wrong direction, so we had a meeting and agreed that for an hour's lesson, a teacher would need no more than six slides. Anything superfluous, like a slide saying 'turn to your chat partner', had to go. We had to work smarter, not harder.
>
> For all the challenges the Covid-19 pandemic presented, it also gave us an opportunity to explore how to do things differently. As you'll know, marking books takes a considerable amount of time for teachers. When we couldn't

> maintain the same rhythm with this due to lockdowns, we had to think about things differently.
>
> This prompted us to ask why we were marking all these books and who we were doing it for. Was it for the parents? The children? Ofsted? From there, we asked, 'Who *should* we be doing this for?' This led to a discussion that changed the way in which books get marked. We now use peer marking, self-marking and marking in lessons as a matter of course. This means that when books do get taken away it is much quicker, and the process is one of acknowledgement rather than detailed marking.
>
> Both of these changes have significantly improved the work-life balance for everyone on our team.

The mantra of working smarter not harder applies to all of us. By developing my senior leadership team and middle managers, I have a lot more support than I did when I started in this role. We share the workload between us, allowing all of us to work smarter.

On my journey as a head, I started out leading from the front, but now I'm growing new leaders who feel empowered to bring new ideas to the table and work on improving our school. I find this incredibly exciting and, to be honest, the ideas they come in with are amazing. I wouldn't be able to come up with half of them on my own!

Our team has come up with some crazy ideas – like a Year 6 sleepover to celebrate the end of the year, where we had 90 children under canvas on the field, with a campfire and games – but some of those have been wildly successful. My view is that as long as the children are safe and learning, I'm willing to try any ideas that come my way. If I'm feeling cautious about implementing something new, this is the benchmark I use. That way, any changes we make are about what's best for our school, our pupils and our families. It's one of the ways I stop myself from making excuses to not try new things.

Sustaining excellence for brighter futures

Sustaining excellence is just as challenging as the journey there, and being reflective has been key for us to maintain this standard, particularly following the disruption caused by Covid-19. As I shared earlier with our changes to PE sessions, the pandemic even gave us unexpected opportunities to improve what we were doing.

When I started at Stanton, I promised myself I would take the school from 'good' to 'outstanding', even though I had no real idea how I would do it. Now, 17 years on, I find myself in the wonderful position of working to make an outstanding school even more outstanding.

Those 17 years have been an incredible journey, and one of the things I'm most proud of is the ethos within our school of seeking continuous improvement. Ours is a job that's never done – both as teachers and headteachers. It doesn't finish once we've trained our team in expectations for excellence. It doesn't finish when a cohort of children move on to the next stage in their education. But it's a job I wouldn't change for the world.

A common analogy for all of us is spinning plates. Being the only person keeping an eye on all the spinning plates in your school is challenging to say the least, if not impossible! We need our teams to help us keep an eye on these plates. At Stanton, we've found the peer observations of lessons have been particularly valuable because they allow everyone to contribute to sustaining excellence in their own way.

It is evident the staff have bought into the no-excuses culture, from their contribution of new ideas to build on good practice and their willingness to share their thoughts at meetings, to discussing a new idea or initiative they would like to lead. They like the consistency of expectations and knowing there is always an opportunity to evolve. They also like knowing we will make changes if something can be done better, such as reviewing the marking policy to make it have value but not be as time consuming. Sharing progress data and small wins, and seeing the positive impact across the school for all our children reinforces that the no-excuses culture does pay off.

When you empower your staff, they will maintain that culture alongside you. When you bring everyone on the journey to 'outstanding', they all contribute in their own way. There's one word that has come up multiple times in this chapter, and that's *consistency*. As heads we have to find the balance between maintaining consistency for our children and adapting to ensure they have the best possible learning environment.

There will always be challenges in the education system. We won't always be able to give our children all the experiences we'd like them to have. But I've found it helpful to focus on ensuring all our children get a taste of what life can offer them when you work hard, play hard and are happy. Working in challenging catchment areas has reaffirmed to me that while children may need additional support, and possibly more time, they all deserve opportunity.

If we use a child's personal situation – where they live, their home life, their personal circumstances – as excuses for a child to not make progress, I feel we're letting that child down. We all like to believe we never give up on children, but if we look across our school system and what's in the media we can find their circumstances are often used as an excuse, which is ultimately also saying they don't deserve the best education. Reading that may feel uncomfortable, but when we think about it, every time we make excuses, or let other people make excuses, for children not achieving, this is essentially what we're saying.

Having a positive mindset and belief is the antidote to this, and the key to moving towards a no-excuses culture. That means when we see a barrier to a child's learning, we highlight this with our teams and take ownership to make the changes in our school. This doesn't have to come from me (or you) as a headteacher. What I've realised is that by instilling, and recruiting to, that positive mindset in everyone in the school, when someone sees a problem or an exciting opportunity to do better they take action. We are an intelligent, skilled and practically minded profession – these are amazing qualities that we can apply to the challenges both we as educators and our children face. I truly believe that by harnessing our natural talents, excellence is achievable for all.

It's easy to say these children are working below where they need to be for their age. It's easy to point to circumstances outside our control, like funding. It's easy to accept 90% of the team doing what we need them to do, while telling ourselves it's just not possible to get 100%.

It's not always easy to challenge those beliefs and let go of the excuses. But our school is a testament to what children from all backgrounds can achieve if we don't let those excuses hinder learning.

The power of no excuses

All children deserve the best education that we can provide them. I'm sure as educators we all agree on that. Giving them opportunities, experiences and high-quality education with high expectations is key to delivering this. We want education to be fun and exciting. We want schools to be places where children can explore and gain knowledge.

Along the way, their wellbeing and more will benefit. Some children will discover the arts for the first time, maybe music, singing or dancing. For others, it will be sport and playing a team game that captivates them. This isn't just about the thrill of the win, but also the enjoyment of participating and working together as a team. Through understanding each other, they discover who they are.

Yes, they'll make mistakes. Yes, they won't always achieve perfect scores. But they will discover that success is sometimes about making a mistake and learning from it, which is often a more valuable lesson than getting everything right the first time.

When we became the fourth most improved school in England and Wales from 2008 to 2012, the recognition of the work that went into those four years was worth the effort. When you get 'outstanding' from Ofsted, you know that means all the work you've put in has been recognised as a success. But as great as an 'outstanding' rating is, what really matters is the journey that you take these children, and staff, on and how successful they become at the other end.

TOP TIPS

- ★ Reflect honestly on your current beliefs about how successful the children at your school can be. Are you falling into the trap of making excuses based on demographics?
- ★ Set clear expectations for your teachers and focus on quality-first methodology to create positive learning environments at every level in your school.
- ★ Keep looking for opportunities to work smarter, not harder. Could you implement some of the changes we have, such as changing the way in which books are marked?

Chapter 4:
The transformation journey – Paul Murphy

Meet Paul...

Paul Murphy is the headteacher at Lancasterian Primary School, which is a larger than average school serving a diverse population. Paul describes the transformation journey as more of a 'messy scribble' than a linear process. He and his team have embarked on a transformation programme that took their school from the bottom of their borough in 2015 to being judged 'outstanding' in all but one area in 2023.

About Lancasterian Primary School

	School	National average
Pupils with a SEND Education, Health and Care Plan	3.5%	2.5%
Pupils with SEND support	14.8%	13.5%
Pupils whose first language is not English	69.8%	22.0%
Pupils eligible for free school meals at any time during the past six years	47.1%	25.9%

In December 2015, I went to see *The Martian*. I was just a few months into my headship at Lancasterian Primary, and a quote from the movie really resonated with the situation I found myself in – one term into a headship at a school that was pretty much at rock bottom.

'At some point, everything's gonna go south on you... and you're going to say "This is it. This is how I end." Now you can either accept that or you can get to work. That's all it is. You just begin. You do the math. You solve one problem... and you solve the next one... and then the next. And if you solve enough problems, *you get a "good" to "outstanding" school*.'[1]

Okay, I admit that I changed the end of the quote! (For those who are curious, it actually ends with, 'you get to come home.') But when I took on my role in September 2015, that was how I had to approach it – one problem at a time. And believe me when I say there were many problems.

What I'm going to share with you here is the rollercoaster journey we've been on at Lancasterian Primary, in the hope that some of what I've learned may help you navigate the peaks and troughs of your transformation journey, whatever that looks like for your school.

The transformation rollercoaster

As a school leader, particularly in the early years of my headship, I sat through too many talks from school leaders that made me feel really inadequate, as they painted a perfect picture of success that sounded like a nice linear progression. However, I think we all know success actually looks more like a messy scribble – you go up, down, back and forth, you loop the loop, and suddenly you feel like you're right back to where you started.

My journey as a head has been like a rollercoaster. Sometimes I'm screaming in fear (not literally) and having a horrendous time. Sometimes I'm screaming in delight (also not literally) and having a really good time.

---

1   *The Martian*, (2015), directed by Ridley Scott, distributed by 20th Century Fox.

But within education there is still the 'super head' narrative – someone who can come in and turn a school around in just five minutes. They then ride off into the sunset, moving onto the next school. I'm sure I'm not alone in wanting to challenge this belief. Real and sustainable change in a school environment isn't down to just one person, and it doesn't happen overnight.

Perhaps even more importantly, we can't rely on 'super heads' if we want any improvement they bring to continue after they leave their position. Really, we are all 'super heads' in our own ways – committed leaders who are trying to do the best for our schools and the communities we serve. Let me explain the level of transformation that was required at Lancasterian Primary when I joined as head, and then I'll share some of the strategies we used to completely change our school's culture.

The only way is up

Our school is in the heart of Tottenham, in one of the most disadvantaged areas of the country. That brings its own sets of opportunities and challenges – I prefer to focus on the opportunities. The kids are fantastic and keep the job interesting. We have incredible diversity in our community and among our staff. Some days we feel like we're getting paid to be part of a brilliant comedy show. Other days we feel a deep sense of fulfilment from helping children and families learn, grow and improve their life chances.

That said, I became the head at Lancasterian Primary at a time of great challenge. I was the fourth headteacher over a two-year period. So many changes in leadership had created a lot of instability and uncertainty for staff, children and families.

The results at the school at the time were very low. We were in the bottom 10% nationally in most areas. We were the lowest performing school at key stage 2 in our local authority. We also had an Ofsted data dashboard from the year before I joined the school. Under the strength section of that data dashboard, it simply said, 'There are no strengths in this data set.'

The only way was up. And there were many things that we needed to work on immediately.

Recruitment became a big priority, particularly strong recruitment at leadership level. Putting in place good performance management systems was crucial to ensure people understood what we wanted from them and that we were able to hold them to account. This included dealing with difficult capability issues and putting support and challenge plans in place where needed.

Clearly, there was work to do on the curriculum. We needed to find the right kind of curriculum for the school – one that continues to develop all the time, but also that's appropriate for our intake of children. It had to be a curriculum from a trusted source that could be adopted quickly.

Training for staff was another priority. We needed to start upskilling staff and helping them to feel more confident to deliver the curriculum that we were putting in place. Making sure that staff had the right resources, including IT resources, was also important.

However, from my perspective, the area that we needed to work on more than anything else was the school culture. I knew that if we could get this right, everything else would follow.

The pain of change and transition

As you well know, even if no work has consciously been done to form a school culture, that doesn't mean there isn't a culture in place. In our case, the culture badly needed to change. However, during the transition period from one culture to the other, pupils inevitably wanted to test the boundaries. Behaviour dipped. It felt like we were going backwards. But I and the rest of my team knew if we held firm in our commitment to our new culture, we would not only accelerate forward but we'd surpass where we had been before.

Of course, this isn't easy. Change can be a painful process – not everyone will be able to keep up with the school's new direction. This can create dilemmas, as you are faced with the need to balance supporting people on your teams with meeting the needs of the children.

It can't be a case of simply dismissing staff that aren't up to the job and hiring new ones. This is stressful for everyone involved, potentially unfair and costly for the school. However, if individuals are not able to meet expectations, the children's needs must come first. Unless we handle this with integrity, supporting staff to meet expectations, and helping people to move on if they can't, can be tricky.

This, of course, is difficult enough normally. When a school is struggling, like ours was, or there is a lot to be desired regarding culture, it is only more difficult. But as my school's journey shows, it is far from impossible.

Key culture indicators

Jo has already done a great job in chapter 2 of explaining what we mean by the term 'culture' and highlighting the importance of a strong culture that runs through every part of school life. The way I like to describe the importance of a school's culture is likening it to baking a cake – bear with me!

To bake a cake, you need to have the best ingredients. In our context, that's the people and resources we have available in our school. You also need the right-shaped, non-stick cake tin – this represents the school improvement strategies that provide the guardrails for everyone to work within. Then you need the oven, which represents the school buildings, facilities and learning environment.

But even if you have the best ingredients and the right cake tin, if you don't get the temperature right in your oven, your cake won't rise. The temperature represents the culture. It runs through and supports everything else. It has the power to help a school succeed or to scupper your best efforts for improvement.

When I joined Lancasterian Primary, a range of indicators showed our culture wasn't where it needed to be. These included:

- **Data** – I've already shared just how bad the data looked. There were no strengths listed on our inspection dashboard, but there was a litany of weaknesses. But at least we had a starting point, even if it was at the very bottom.

- **Language** – Language was challenging. The way staff communicated with each other was sometimes less than desirable, and this highlighted an 'us and them' culture. Many difficult conversations were needed, and sometimes our teachers did not take this well.
- **Beliefs** – I inherited issues between staff and leadership. Small challenges quickly became big issues, and staff were quick to go to the union. (I used to joke that if I wanted to open a window, I'd have to contact the union to get permission!)
- **History** – As I mentioned, I was the fourth head in a two-year period, which probably explains a lot of the challenges. This made it very difficult for staff to trust me, so I made a point of telling people I would stay for at least six years to not only build trust that I was in it for the long haul, but also to keep myself accountable.
- **Habits and behaviours** – The school was like a ghost town at around 4pm every day, just 30 minutes after the kids had left. I discovered that when taking on a new class, many teachers would clear out the classroom at the start of the school year, not the beginning of the summer holidays. What's more, they'd just bag everything up and leave it outside the classroom for the site team to deal with. This seemingly small thing spoke to issues around the hierarchy, taking responsibility and delegation.

When we're in the day-to-day of school life, it can be easy to miss these indicators. By looking at those key indicators, it was clear we had a lot of work to do around culture, in particular our vision and values, if we were going to move the school forward.

> What data, language, beliefs, history, habits and behaviours support your culture? Which don't?

Transforming a school

When faced with so many challenges, where do you even start? We found that the area that had the most impact early on, and that continues to have the greatest impact on our school's culture, was the work we did around our vision and values. When I took on Lancasterian Primary, there was a vision, but nobody knew what it was or could explain it.

I even struggled to find it on our website. There were some shared values around inclusion, but they weren't specifically named and, as with the vision, no one could really talk about them in great depth.

I knew that getting our vision and values right was essential in moving the culture forward quickly. So, my senior leadership team and I worked with Sonia for five and a half days to develop the vision and values together.

Our vision

This is our vision at Lancasterian Primary:

> **We will make a fairer society**
>
> A society where everyone can reach the top of the mountain because all of us understand that achieving ambitions includes learning from mistakes.
>
> A society where everyone has the skills and knowledge to open any door because all of us break down barriers to opportunity.
>
> A society where everyone improves the world we share because all of us see creative solutions to the issues we face together.
>
> **To do this, we'll make the best school**
>
> A school where every child embraces learning as a demanding lifelong journey, because all of us show them how to love challenge and growth.
>
> A school where every child feels proud of who they are and their own uniqueness because all of us celebrate difference.
>
> And a school where every child leaves the gate with fond memories, a creative outlook and a sense of excitement for the road ahead, because all of us have put them at the centre of everything we do.

There are two key themes that run through our vision:

1. **Creating a fairer society** – We want to make sure we give the children the greatest chance of success, regardless of their starting point. We want to get them ready for the next stage of their education in every sense, by helping them get excited about learning and making sure they love coming to school and want to continue.

2. **Being the best school** – Being an average school isn't going to work for the children we teach. Their needs are too high for us to just do an average job, so we have to be the best we can be for them.

You can see that we've used a lot of imagery and emotive language in our vision. We wanted to paint a picture in the mind of whoever reads or hears our vision and make them feel proud of who we are. But creating a vision is just the first step – it's nothing if it's not shared in such a way that everyone who's part of the school knows it and wants to be a part it.

Hitting home

It's one thing to share your vision, but it's another for it to really land with your team. After working on the school's vision, I was ready to share it on our January inset days. I spent a lot of time during the Christmas holiday rehearsing a speech that I'd written with Sonia and the team. I wanted to get it right.

The way in which I presented was different from what the staff at my school were used to, so that helped to engage them straight off the bat. After I'd introduced the vision, all the staff had a chance to discuss it, and the feedback was overwhelmingly positive. Even a member of staff who was usually critical was fully onboard, which gave everyone confidence.

Once I had the staff on board, it was time to bring the children with us. We introduced the vision in an assembly, breaking it down into six main segments. As you know, getting children to engage with something like this can be tricky, so we ran a drawing competition to get them excited. Over the next six weeks, we got the children to draw pictures related to each part of the vision, which we then used to create a vision poster. We still use that poster to this day.

Finally, we shared it with our parents and wider community by focusing on different parts of the vision in our newsletter over a series of months. We also held coffee mornings and invited parents so we could talk them through the vision. It's also on prominent display in our school foyer and on our website.

Here are a few little tricks we came up with to help make sure everyone in our school saw our vision wherever they went:

- We put it on the home screen of all the school's desktop computers, so the vision is the first thing anyone sees when they log in.
- We start every staff training session with the vision and ask staff to identify which part of the vision we'll be working towards during that meeting.
- We put the vision on the back of staff lanyards so it's with people every day. We wanted to embed the vision as something that's always present with them.
- We run standalone training sessions around the vision, which may last an hour or so. For example, we've done human freeze frames, where teams have to make a freeze frame to communicate one part of the vision.

Our vision is a constant part of our dialogue. We refer to it when giving praise, and when evaluating our decisions. It helps us structure and frame both positive and challenging conversations, making everything about the school and what's best for our pupils.

The values behind behavioural change

As Sonia aptly puts it, 'Culture is behaviour over time.' In other words, the behaviours you promote or accept become the culture of the school. As heads, our job is to promote positive behaviour while dealing with negative behaviour – easier said than done, as many of you know! In our school, we wanted to not only change the behaviour of the children, but also the staff and the parents. There's nothing like a big challenge!

With the vision set out, it was time to turn our attention to our values, because we needed to be able to explain these in order to create a solid foundation for our behaviours as children and adults alike. Our first challenge was to identify just six values from a very long list.

After much discussion, we eventually agreed on:

- Inclusion.
- Lifelong learning.
- Growth mindset.
- Integrity.
- High aspirations.
- Respect.

Once we'd agreed these values, we had to find a way to bring them to life. Again working with Sonia, we did this through creative writing – if you've never thought about doing something similar then I definitely recommend it as an exercise. It really has transformed our school.

Rolling out the values for staff

The senior leadership team, along with the chair of our governors, created a narrative for each of our values. I'm not going to lie, initially some of our senior leadership team thought this was a little bit crazy, but to their credit they stuck with it. The result was that, instead of just saying, 'One of our values is inclusion and this means [insert standard, unengaging dictionary definition here]', we had either a short story, a poem or a song for every value that we could share with the whole team.

When we introduced these to the rest of our staff, we saw how important it was to have brought these values to life. They weren't just words on a page; they were values that everyone deeply understood and remembered.

Here's an example of what we created for 'Integrity':

If every day
You can honestly say
Once you step through our door you are true

If in each interaction
(And not just a fraction)
It's the same – what you say and you do

If in both work and play
You are what you say
And you always stick to your word

If alignment is neat
Through head, mouth, heart and feet
And your values are always heard

If you're humble and fair
And there's no ego there
And you always come back to your scruples

Then integrity's yours
Trust will open up doors
Because you do what you do for the pupils

Rolling out the values for pupils

Once we had the narratives for each value, we took that a step further to help all our children really engage with and remember them. We created a character for each of our six values and worked with a graphic designer to visually bring them to life. To give credit where it's due, this idea was born after I'd visited a fantastic school with Sonia, Surrey Square Primary School. Investing in a graphic designer for this work has been more than worth the expense. These value characters have become one of the strongest parts of our school marketing.

Here's Imari Inclusion, and this is his story.

Imari Inclusion loves getting everyone involved. With his eight arms, he's always ready to help others.

He loves to explore his environment, seeking out new friends. As a really caring value, he's quick to offer a hug or kind word to those who may feel vulnerable or upset. He will share his toys and equipment with others to cheer them up and help them to play games together well. He knows that taking turns is so important and he loves to sing out, 'Show you care, play fair!'

Imari's most special possession is his wonderful jar of treasured shapes. They come in all different sizes, forms, colours and patterns. They can all do different things individually, but when they come together they create dazzling results. They remind him of everyone at school, all their unique differences and how remarkable they can be when they are together. He loves to play with them all.

> Imari knows that we're all different with our own strengths, weaknesses, interests and personalities. That's what makes us all special. He celebrates our unique cultures and beliefs with the beautiful, contrasting patterns on each of his arms. He's so proud of them and how they come together to make him unique.

In the first year, we rolled these out, one value per month. Now that they're thoroughly embedded as part of the school, we include the values characters as part of the sequence of learning. The children cover one value every half term, every year. They also all receive a booklet about the values families when they start at our school.

In addition, when we want to talk to the children about things that are happening in school, either with learning or their behaviour, we do it through our values. We may say, 'Well done, what you did was just like Imari Inclusion!' or if they're in trouble we could ask, 'What would Imari Inclusion do in this situation?' Sometimes you get a begrudging answer in the latter situation, but they know what the right behaviour is!

> At the end of every half term, each class identifies their values ambassador. This ambassador gets a badge that shows they're the ambassador for that value for their class. There are even rewards, assigned by the teachers, for pupils who are most improved in a particular value each half term.

Rolling out the values for parents

We then got a little bit carried away and created parent characters with these values too. I say we got carried away, but we actually made a conscious decision to take this approach after realising our parents didn't know our values as well as the children or staff did.

We wanted some of our parents to be involved in this process, so we put together a working party of parents and explained what we wanted to do. We asked them how they'd show each of the values as a parent, and what models of families we should include to represent our school. We were amazed and incredibly happy with what they came back with.

Our values parents are:

- A mum and dad.
- A mum and step-dad, with differing cultural heritages.
- Grandparents.
- Foster carers.
- A single mum.
- A gay couple (two mums).

Just as with the values characters, each set of parents has their own story. Here is the story that accompanies Ignacio's carers, the Integrity Family.

Ignacio's Carers — The Integrity Family

Ignacio lives with his foster carers, and they bring him to Lancasterian Primary School because they want him to understand the importance of doing the right thing.

> Just like Ignacio, they are honest through and through, from the top of their ears to the tip of their tails. They tell the truth when working with the school to sort out problems.
>
> They are dependable members of our school community and bring Ignacio to school on time, every day, unless he is too ill to come in.
>
> We all make mistakes in our behaviour occasionally, and Ignacio's carers always make sure to say sorry when they make mistakes so Ignacio is encouraged to do the same. They wave their tails to remind him of this powerful word.
>
> Their strong and sturdy legs do not allow others' negativity to sway or influence their relationship with the school. They choose what they THINK, FEEL, SAY and DO for themselves.
>
> Ignacio's carers always remember to share their praise balloon with Ignacio when he is true to his values. They challenge him when he is not.

We give our parents a booklet of these stories when their children join the school, which allows them to see what we expect of them from the start and showcases the diverse family models we have within our community.

Embedding our values everywhere

We haven't stopped with booklets and teaching though. We changed the school's signage to showcase our values families, and we changed our entryway so you see them as you walk into school. They're in the foyer, the school hall and every classroom. They regularly feature in our newsletters, they're on the website and we talk about them at our coffee mornings. They are there for all to see.

Since we introduced our values families, we've developed how we use them every year. We ask our house captains what they want to do with the values each year. As examples of what they've come up with, we've had dress-up days and even a competition similar to 'Who Wants to Be a Millionaire?' around the values. The following are just some of the other approaches that we've found effective for embedding our values in the fabric of our school culture.

Journey books

Every child is given a 'journey book' in Year 1. They fill this in throughout each school year, covering one value per half term. As part of this exercise, they score themselves against each of our values and the associated behaviours. This book travels with them all the way through to Year 6 and is a way for them to track their journey through our school. We encourage the children to write a narrative or draw a picture to show when they've embodied that value, both in and outside of school.

Values cards

We have also introduced 'values cards', which is another idea I got from visiting a school with Sonia. The idea is that anyone can give anyone else in the school a value card, and when you give someone a value card you explain why. We often have a competition associated with our values cards. For example, last year we said that anyone who managed to get 25 value cards within the year would go into a draw to win a bike.

> ### Sharing external recognition
>
> It can take time for these cultural changes to have the desired effect, so I felt it was really important that I could show people things were moving in the right direction, even if they were moving really slowly.
>
> Early in our journey I tried as much as possible to get that external recognition for our staff. I did things like inviting the local authority assistant director for schools and learning to visit the school. When any person who visited our school fed back to me verbally, I'd make sure they also put their feedback in an email to me.
>
> This gave me something I could pass on to staff. Sometimes I could take quotes from it and put it in the newsletter for parents. As a result, I was sharing the positive things people were saying about the school with the community, rather than just keeping them at the head or senior leadership level.

Impact on outcomes

As I covered earlier in this chapter, when I became the headteacher, we were at the bottom of the borough in terms of KS2 outcomes. Nationally, we were in the bottom 10% in most outcomes from Reception to Year 6, with very few positives to talk about in the data. I only mention this again to show just how far we have come. We have moved from that low point to being at least in line with national outcomes.

In many areas we are now above national outcomes, and we performed particularly well in the first SATs tests following the Covid-19 pandemic. This was an even greater achievement in my view than exceeding national outcomes because it meant we got through the pandemic without taking the massive hit on outcomes we were worried about. The strategies we used to achieve this all came about as part of the process of changing the culture of the school.

But not all the positive outcomes we've seen have been about our results. In 2023, we absolutely bombed in our KS2 reading performance because it was such a challenging paper and a lot of our children who speak English as an additional language couldn't finish it. After a five-year trend of improvement in our Year 6 outcomes, this sudden dip was very demoralising for the community. However, we had to hold on to our vision and remember our value of 'growth mindset', and we came to understand that this dip didn't mean we were back to square one.

As a school, the difference is that it only took us one year to get back on track. We're not having to embark on another five-year journey to get our results up towards the national average again – but we are still riding that rollercoaster!

Impact on behaviour

As I'm sure many of you do, we classify the severity of behaviour consequences in our school in stages, with stage three being the most serious. I've tracked our stage three incidents since I started with the school, and you can see how dramatically the picture has changed since we introduced our vision and values in the following graph. I've only included the autumn term's data here because that is the only term that wasn't impacted by the Covid-19 pandemic in recent years.

Impact on behaviour

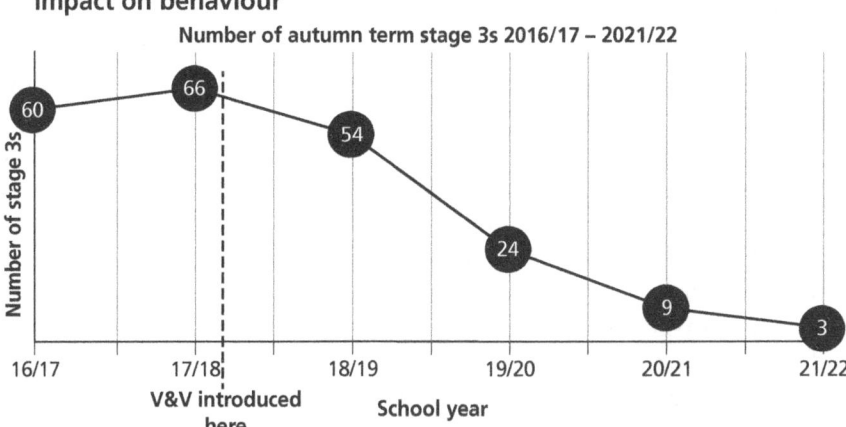

From this, it's clear to see that our vision and values have helped the children understand what we want and expect in terms of their behaviour for learning and their interactions with one another.

> The values are a big part of conversations that we have, particularly when faced with difficulties. In one staff meeting, we were talking about a child we were really struggling with. We identified that we had a hard decision to make, because we had two values clashing: we wanted to include that child, but there were other children getting hurt. It was a respect issue. Knowing our values so well helps us work through those difficult issues.

A note about Ofsted

When we eventually had an Ofsted inspection – which came two years later than expected – we were rated 'outstanding' in four out of the five areas, and our values were referenced several times in the report.

- 'Leaders have established a set of values that are central to the life of the school.'
- 'Pupils learn about important issues in a positive and inclusive culture, which is informed by the school's values.'
- 'Leaders work in developing people's resilience and respect for others is exceptional.'

It was great to see that this was picked up by the inspectors who came to the school – definitely one of the happy times on our rollercoaster.

That said, we had to fight to get 'outstanding' in leadership and management – initially, they rated us 'good'. When I saw the initial report, I thought, *'No way.'* I'd sat in on the middle leader meetings and I knew how amazing these leaders are. There was a ton of evidence, so we fought it by going through the stage one and stage two complaints process to get it changed. The reason I'm sharing this is because if you don't agree with what an Ofsted inspector is telling you, you can push back. These inspectors are human beings giving their subjective opinion, and they can be flawed. So don't be afraid to fight if you really believe you deserve better and can back up your opinion.

We all know that Ofsted isn't ideal. It's a problematic system due to its dated and flawed nature. It's dated because it's a top-down approach to evaluating school performance, which is not how we work with our staff to identify their strengths and areas for development. And it's flawed because it's too dependent on the subjective views of individual inspectors. There are many instances where an individual perspective on how a school should be run has negatively impacted schools. Although I agree schools should be held accountable, I don't believe that the current Ofsted model is the best way to do so.

Impact on staff

We run a staff satisfaction survey twice a year in which staff are asked whether they really agree, agree, disagree or really disagree with a number of statements, including the following four:

1. I like the direction the school is currently taking.
2. I am committed to the school's vision.
3. I am optimistic about the future success of the school.
4. I am happy and fulfilled in my role at the school.

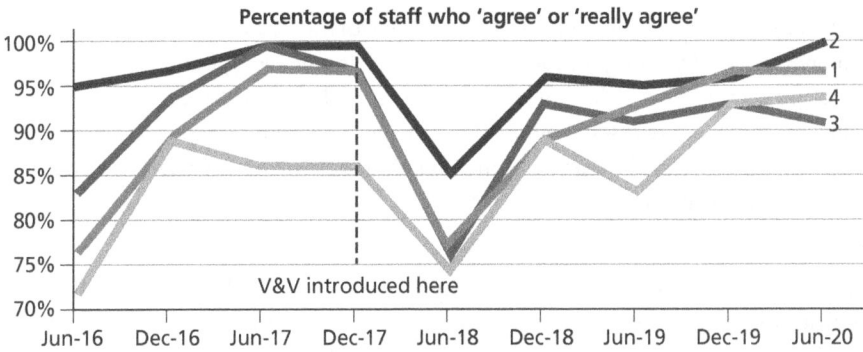

What I found interesting (although at the time it was scary!) was that in the period immediately after we introduced the vision and values we had a significant dip in staff satisfaction. A number of teachers left the school that year – it was definitely a terrifying drop on our rollercoaster ride. But in every challenge, there is opportunity, and this actually turned out to be positive.

A number of the staff who left weren't on board with the new direction the school was taking, and they weren't putting in a lot of discretionary effort. Without wishing to sound harsh, they were doing a mediocre job rather than stepping up and doing the outstanding job we needed them to do. I can only thank them for leaving, because in doing so they gave us the space to recruit new staff who fully bought into our vision and values. This was a massive turning point.

Since this time, we've embedded our vision and values in our performance management by creating three objectives:

- **High inspiration** – which is to do with the children's outcomes.
- **Growth mindset** – which is about improving something you're currently struggling with.
- **Lifelong learning** – which involves taking on something new.

> We host an annual staff conference where we take staff away for two days using money raised by charging for parking spaces in our playground for Tottenham Hotspurs football matches on the weekends and during the evenings. During this conference, we discuss what it feels like to work at the school and how they think it feels for the children. We often find that our values are referenced during these conversations.

We also have 'staff values journeys', which were developed with our whole team at one of our annual conferences. These are similar to the children's journey books, and this tool allows each member of staff to score themselves on five behaviours linked to each of our values. They fill in these scorecards ahead of their performance management check-ins and can then have a values-based discussion with their line manager about their strengths and what they need to work on. Because they came up with the idea and created the process, they are holding themselves accountable.

We've also done loads of work around psychological safety in the school. We wanted to create an organisational culture where knowledge and innovation can flourish because people feel safe to speak their minds and put their ideas forward.

I highly recommend the book, *The Fearless Organization*, by Amy C. Edmondson, and there's one quote in particular that stands out for me:

> Making dramatic, systemic change happen is highly dependent on building psychological safety that allows employees to speak up with their concerns and ideas for improvement, as well as to experiment in small ways to figure out what works best.[2]

Impact on recruitment

Another thing that's been absolutely key is embedding our culture in the recruitment strategy. By simply sharing the two main themes of our vision – that we make a fairer society by ensuring all children are secondary ready, and that we have to be the *best* school to achieve this,

---

2   Edmondson, A. C. (2018). *The Fearless Organization: Creating psychological safety in the workplace for learning, innovation, and growth.*

not just do an average job – we are able to help people decide whether our school is a good fit for them.

If this part of our vision puts them off applying, that's fine. But if it makes them excited about working for our school, we already know they are likely to be the right kind of people to contribute to our school culture. This is why our vision and values are included in the recruitment pack, are part of our interview questions and are an essential part of the induction process.

Vision and values: the beating heart of our school culture

Although we've made a lot of incredible progress at Lancasterian Primary, the work is never done. We've transformed from a school that was very demoralised and providing poor outcomes for our children and wider community to one that is values-driven with a strong vision for a better future. I hope you can see that while we have come a long way, our journey has been far from linear.

There have been many difficult times. We've experienced dips in our results, and we certainly haven't seen any overnight improvements. However, I believe all the hard work has been more than worth the effort.

I'd just like to leave you with the reminder that this really is a rollercoaster. I'm sure you'll agree that sometimes being a headteacher is the best job in the world, and at other times it's the worst job in the world. But with a guiding vision and strong values, we can ride out the lows and make it back to the highs.

TOP TIPS

★ Build a clear picture of your starting point and start your journey from there. Accept that change can take time and be painful. Sometimes things need to get worse before they get better.

★ Create a strong vision and values to underpin your culture. Find creative ways to bring those values to life for everyone in your school community – from the pupils and staff to the parents. Feel free to steal any of the ideas I've shared with you here!

★ Provide as much recognition as you can on this journey to keep everyone motivated and highlight the progress you've made. We can't avoid challenges – it's part of the job – but we can choose the mindset we approach them with as individuals and as a team.

Chapter 5:
From challenges to opportunities – Maxine Low

Meet Maxine...

Maxine Low is the headteacher at Brooklands Farm Primary School in Milton Keynes. It is a huge, six-form entry primary school with over 1,350 pupils, many of whom speak English as an additional language. Maxine fought for the inception of this school to support the local community and has led it since it opened in 2010. Her approach is to deliver smart education with a heart.

About Brooklands Farm Primary School

	School	National average
Pupils with a SEND Education, Health and Care Plan	1.3%	2.5%
Pupils with SEND support	15.4%	13.5%
Pupils whose first language is not English	53%	22.0%
Pupils eligible for free school meals at any time during the past six years	10.2%	25.9%

People often ask me why I became a headteacher. My answer is surprisingly simple; it's because I'm a learner and I want to be an advocate. That's what drives me. Advocacy became my passion during my first headship at a nursery school.

The school was underneath a tower block, with a Sure Start centre attached to it. I felt I was up to the challenge. But the story I want to tell you about my first headship isn't about the school, but about someone who lived very close by – my Aunty Catherine.

Aunty Catherine lived on the tenth floor of the tower block above the school. To say my aunt and I had taken different paths in life would be an understatement. While I had become a headteacher, Aunty Catherine faced personal challenges that were socially and emotionally complex, and painful. Yet despite this, her advocacy shone.

I noticed that all the women who lived in the tower block would go to Aunty Catherine with their problems – this included domestic violence, extreme poverty or needing support with their childcare. She had become their advocate. She would be their voice when they couldn't speak out themselves.

Sometimes Aunty Catherine would come downstairs, knock on the door of my school and ask, 'Is Maxine there?' My staff would turn her away, telling her I wasn't. Then they'd come to me and tell me they couldn't believe she was my aunt.

That was when I became passionate about being an advocate for those who couldn't be heard. I decided that if they wouldn't let my Aunty Catherine into the school, I would be an advocate for her and the people she represented. If someone would let me into a room, as a headteacher, I would bring the voices of my community with me, because they need to be heard so we can make a difference.

In this chapter, I'm going to share how this ethos of being an advocate and lifelong learner has resulted in a culture of innovation within our school.

Identifying challenges

We are living in a context where change is constant. Leaders have to constantly adapt to what's happening in the wider world, the politics within our country and communities and in their classrooms, as Paul explained in chapter 4. This requires us as school leaders to have a multilayered lens that allows us to see all the challenges we are facing in the school system.

It is only when we are able to see this holistic view of the challenges we face that we are able to effectively prioritise them. But sometimes challenges can be hidden from us as headteachers. They may be things that we don't immediately see, but they are nonetheless challenges that those working in our classrooms and more closely interacting with the children face regularly. As leaders, we therefore need to create a culture that is open, honest and has no blame attached to it. This encourages the people within our organisations to come forward and share their voices.

As you and I both know, this can be easier said than done. But the benefits of creating that culture of psychological safety can't be overstated. We all benefit when people feel free to speak up. The minute everyone in our schools has the confidence to share with us, our path forward becomes clearer. When challenges become evident, we are able to make better informed decisions about how we're going to prioritise those challenges, what resources we may need and what networks and collaborations we may need to build to ensure we are facing the challenges with the right tools.

We won't even look for solutions if we don't know a challenge exists. This is why creating this safe and open culture is so crucial, especially if we all want to lead exceptional schools that recognise the difference we need to make in the world.

If, as headteachers, we were able to focus solely on our schools and what our wider communities needed, I'm sure many of us would do things differently to the way in which we do them. But our education system doesn't allow, in my view, enough flexibility around problem solving. We're constantly reading in the media about what a Labour government would do or what a Conservative government would do. Somehow, we have to balance these often-competing political priorities with what we want to do for the best of our schools and pupils.

On top of that, it seems no one (at the time of writing) is really talking openly about what the Covid-19 pandemic has done to our education system and how it's affected children's behaviour. I believe that as school leaders, we have to be brave and share our challenges with one another.

After all, working in a school is complex and challenging, and some days completely overwhelming.

But if we don't feel safe enough to share these challenges with one another, we will not only feel alone in our struggles in our schools, but we're also less likely to find effective strategies to tackle the underlying issues. This is also true when it comes to talking about the challenges we face within our teams and schools – we have to bring them into the light. As the saying goes, 'It's good to talk.' But I believe it's better to listen.

The power of holding space

Brooklands Farm Primary school grew rapidly – we went from having 49 pupils to having 1,300 in about 10 years. We started as a two-form entry in the first year, then became a three-form entry in the second year, and by the fifth year we were a six-form entry school across two sites.

As I'm sure you can imagine, the amount of challenge that was coming to the table was colossal and at times overwhelming. In the face of so much change, it was difficult for me to assess what the right solution to any given problem may be. When we started, I didn't know who my community was. I didn't know what challenges they would face. I didn't know who I'd be recruiting as teachers.

The only way that I could identify the challenges was to listen very carefully. To make sure that people at every level of the organisation could tell me what I needed to hear, I had to build a culture where I held a space for everybody. The ability to listen and hold space has served me very well over the years.

Breaking it down

In the first year of my headship, my peers took me on a study week to Reggio Emilia in Italy, where I learned more about the Reggio Emilia Approach to education, which is renowned globally as the best early years provision in the world. I found my pedagogical home! The theories and practices of Malaguzzi, who explored the importance of relationships, listening and co-constructing learning journeys with children who they believe are strong and powerful, has shaped my leadership for 27 years.

However, as you'll know, when schools grow – as ours did – it can be difficult to hear from everyone. After all, there is only one of you and potentially dozens of teachers, not to mention hundreds of pupils. To make sure everyone would continue to be heard at Brooklands as we grew, we had to take an innovative approach. Perhaps this could help you if you are the head of a larger school.

Although we're a six-form entry primary school, I have organised the wider school into a series of smaller 'schools'. Each of these is no bigger than 180 children, and each has its own headteacher. As you'll know, small schools can rise really quickly – and they can drop really quickly. But they can also listen really well. I believe this has been one of the keys to our success as we've grown.

One simple thing we do is 'Tell Me Tuesday'. Every Tuesday, we send out a question via a Google form. The children in each class sit in a circle with their teacher, talk about the question and share what they think the answer could be. These questions are really varied. One week we could ask, 'What do we think about history in this school?' Another week the question could be, 'Does everyone feel safe in this school?' The Google form then collates the data so we can take action that matters.

Then we can take all the data we've gathered across all the classes in the school and share it. We put it up on walls to show what people are saying. Then we explore how we can turn that into actions to benefit everyone.

Listen harder

We all know listening is a key tool for any leader. It's particularly important in a school setting, as it's this skill that helps us identify the challenges our communities are facing.

The way I see it is that, in the simplest of terms, my job is to hold a space. I have to ensure that I never blame somebody for a mistake, that my actions and behaviours are calm and reflective, that I am open and honest and that I'm not scared of making mistakes. This is how I approach leadership.

In alignment with being open and honest, I will often share the mistakes I make so people can see how I recover from them. Managing my own behaviours so that I can mirror and demonstrate the culture that is required in a context where everything is changing, and the challenge is high, is not an easy task. But I've learned that if I don't do those things then I can't listen properly – and as I've discussed, listening properly is crucial to identifying the challenges surrounding us. It's not always easy though. Sometimes we have to work really hard to get people to talk to us.

> ### Everybody's voice matters
>
> At Brooklands, we've found one of the best ways to listen is to carry out lots of surveys. We recently sent out one staff survey that only 47% of staff responded to. So, I recorded a little video explaining why this matters and asking people to come forward and have a voice. I reiterated how immensely important all of their voices were to me.
>
> I tend to see the school community as quite non-hierarchical. My mum was a caretaker. My dad was a cleaner. I've been a teaching assistant, a nursery nurse, a teacher; I've done the midday supervisor's role, and now I'm a head. Everybody's voice matters to me. I want to hear from everyone on our school's team. After I sent that video out, the response rate shot up to 90%. Sometimes giving people an opportunity to make their voices heard isn't enough; we have to demonstrate that we really do want to listen.

One thing I've learned over the years is that your teachers with teaching and learning responsibilities (TLRs) are some of the people who listen the most. They know everything that goes on in a school. As headteachers we may think we know everything that goes on in our schools, but if we want to know what's *really* going on, we need to talk to our TLRs, the people who are middle leaders.

Interestingly, Google has abandoned training sessions for its staff led by senior leaders. Their training sessions are now run through the company's middle leaders. This is just the first of several examples I'll share with you where I've learned new approaches by looking at the business world.

What is clear is that we need to change our leadership approach within education as a whole. Many young teachers joining the profession want leaders who listen and engage with them to improve their organisation. We have to create a new dialogue around leadership in our schools to combat this feeling of not being listened to, and in turn, encourage more young people to join our profession.

To do that, we have to listen to their views (no matter how painful they may be at times) so we can understand their concerns. I am also a big believer in the innovative nature of schools. In fact, there's more innovation in our education system than you may think at first glance.

Connecting listening to innovative problem solving

Teachers innovate every single day. When their students walk into their classrooms, they have to think about what strategy is going to be effective to allow that child to achieve that day. Schools are hotbeds of innovation, and we should celebrate the fact they are places where teachers want to find the best solutions they possibly can for their learners – not just once a year or once a term, but every day.

However, the school system as a whole is very systematic and hierarchical, and it hasn't changed for many years. As a result, innovation within a wider school setting is often seen as too risky. Leaders who are prepared to find innovative solutions and discover new tools and strategies that could solve the problems we face effectively are all too often viewed as reckless. So, while our individual teachers may be innovating on a daily basis, as headteachers we are repeatedly (albeit subtly) told that innovation is 'bad'.

The government funds many of the solutions to the perceived problems in our education system. This means we are obliged to follow their lead, and as a result school leaders often lack the mindset and tools for innovation. They see themselves as public servants, driven by a duty to follow government directives. It's easy to see how we got here.

A prime example is the teaching of phonics, which the government believes will raise reading standards. While this is true, it overlooks the importance of reading for enjoyment. As school leaders, we understand the importance of reading for pleasure. We also know that the real issue isn't decoding or fluency, but rather that children aren't picking up books and reading for fun. They don't know which books they like and are choosing not to read, opting for gaming or social media instead. (Incidentally, Paula has some great tips for encouraging reading for enjoyment in chapter 7.)

If the government were to listen to us and hear about our experiences on the ground, they may be persuaded to take a different approach. But we all know that's not how this works! Instead, the funding is in phonics, and therefore that's where our focus must go. It doesn't help that this is also what Ofsted focuses on, and as public servants we must adhere to this system and rationale. This creates a conflict for us. We are aware of the issues within our schools and want to find innovative and effective solutions, but we are also being told via a top-down approach what the solution should be.

This conflict can cost us our jobs if we don't act as public servants and follow Ofsted's expectations. If we choose to listen to our community, school, classrooms, children and parents, we can risk our positions. Consequently, and very understandably, we are often reluctant to take such risks.

After all, innovation and innovative approaches are seen as being messy. Mess and a strictly structured system are *not* things that go hand in hand. But I strongly disagree that innovation has no place in the school system. I'll share some of the ways in which I've taken risks through innovation at my school later in this chapter.

To help us embrace risk in a healthy way, I've found it's more useful to think of mess (innovation) and a structured system as different ends of the same spectrum. Moving away from the structured end of the spectrum towards the 'messy' end is a journey, and how far you go on that journey will depend on your school and its needs.

The innovation journey

I enjoy innovation. I am comfortable with the messiness and the mistakes that innovation requires. As I've said, I want to challenge the idea that innovation is too messy and dangerous for our school system. Innovation is a process, but it's not always messy in a risky way, especially when there is a framework to manage it.

I've found it particularly helpful to look at business and use project management tools to support people trying out new strategies in our school. These tools allow me to listen better to what those people are experiencing so I can guide the direction we take. My ability to listen during this process makes it safe, but my role goes beyond just listening. I also have to slow down and foster a culture of openness and honesty. In doing so, I give everyone on my team the space they need to find tools to facilitate change.

It has also been helpful in our school to reframe how we think about innovation as a concept. For me, innovation isn't just one great idea that everyone agrees on and moves towards. Rather, innovation is tiny steps towards finding a solution to any problem. Creating a framework around this process allows people to feel safe and know that they are part of a journey. I'll share the framework we use shortly.

I think the word 'journey' is safer within the education system than 'innovation'. In my experience, teachers and other leaders understand it better and feel more comfortable with it. 'We have a challenge, and we need to go on a journey to find a solution' sounds less scary than, 'We need to innovate to find a solution to this problem.'

Building a problem-solving framework

In the past, I have had critics who prefer hierarchical approaches to finding solutions. This means I have had to be discreet about the solutions I have found along my journey. However, by being persistent, tenacious and keeping my head down, I believe that I have begun to build a framework that will keep me and other leaders safe when they are trying to find solutions to future problems.

What follows are the stages of the framework I've developed, and then I'll share an example of how I applied this at Brooklands Farm.

This framework comes in three stages:

- Building your hypothesis and your 'why' with a team to help you.
- Testing your solutions.
- Sharing your solutions with a wider group and monitoring the results.

Building a hypothesis and a team

First, build your hypothesis by listening to others. Use some of the techniques I shared earlier if you feel they'll be helpful in your school. I can assure you that if you have an open and honest culture, the people around you will tell you what the problem is. Listen carefully and build the structures and systems that let you do this.

Next, build your 'why'. Why do we need to go on a journey to find a new solution? Why can't we just carry on doing what we're doing? Ask these questions and see what answers different people give you. It's enlightening! Use what you have learned by listening, combined with evidence and theories, to create a reason to act. This part is important, because we need to be able to communicate not only the journey we'll be taking people on, but also why it matters.

To build your team, look for people who can both cope with change and are motivated to find a new solution. How motivated someone is to find a new solution usually depends on what the problem is and how much that problem affects them and their pupils.

Before we move into finding solutions, there is one more step we take when building a team for this purpose. We listen carefully to each other to learn who the other people on the team are and where they are. I often build a team from a cross section of leaders, teachers, business staff, parents and children so I can listen from lots of different angles. We share our stories and 'why' we want to be there, which builds psychological safety, before we start talking about the problem at hand.

Testing your solutions

Once we all feel safe, we can start searching for solutions. As a team, try out different strategies that all of you think are going to solve the problem. During this process, I listen very carefully so I can monitor whether the solutions being built can be fed into the school system or are too expensive, too resource-heavy or won't be accepted by the DfE or Ofsted. As headteachers, we have a view of the broader education landscape that others may not, so it's important that we assess each solution presented through this lens. This means there may be times when we have to shape the thinking of our team so that a scalable, shareable solution can emerge.

I have also found it invaluable to have a team of people outside of our school who we can turn to for additional support. These are people who are part of my national networks or collaborations, and who I feel safe checking in with to make sure the problems we're seeing at our school are also problems they are seeing. As I said earlier, if one school is seeing an issue, another school is likely seeing the same or a similar issue.

We can start having these conversations with our wider networks while the team within our school is working on finding strategies to solve the challenge. We may even get some new thinking from one of these contacts that can help us see the challenge from a new perspective or arrive at a solution more quickly.

Sharing your solutions

Once we've got some scalable tools or strategies that we can use, we can share them with a bigger group of practitioners. Over the years, we've learned that the way we share is particularly important. At Brooklands, we do this through opening classroom doors so teachers can learn from each other. This has helped everyone in our school community engage with innovation and has ensured our innovation leads to solving real-world problems.

Once the new strategy or tool has been shared, then we will standardise it and set out what implementing it needs to look like. By this stage, we can say with confidence that we have tried these strategies, and this is what has emerged. We can also explain why we want everybody to do things in a certain way. As all of us know, in-school variance is the biggest killer of pupil progress. So, our aim has to be to standardise any strategies we come up with and make them consistent across the school.

As with many elements of educational leadership, this is often easier said than done. Establishing consistency in how solutions are shared is just the starting point. We then have to monitor that consistency, as Helen explained in chapter 3. I've found that one of the most important principles to bear in mind here is making it feel safe for people to try new things.

The way we do this is to go full circle and say, 'Okay, so we use these strategies, we said everybody should use them, but nobody's going to use them in exactly the right way. So, who's using them best?' This isn't about blame; it's about seeing what works in practice. What is the best way to roll this out further? When we discover what works, and have practical evidence to back that up, it becomes much easier to share a solution across the organisation more widely. You could say that in doing so we are lowering the risk in innovation.

Problem solving during the Covid-19 pandemic

During the Covid-19 pandemic, there was a moral imperative that we innovated within the school system. Despite it being a challenge, Covid-19 also gave me an opportunity to use my talents and test my frameworks.

I listened to teachers, children's parents and leaders. I gathered their views on what the struggle was. I did this using a single question, 'How will we ensure all children learn during this period?' I also listened outside my organisation, through networking with lots of leaders nationally to see what kinds of solutions they were finding.

My granddad used to tell me I was a bit of a 'know-all, know-nothing' – I think this is the perfect description of being a head! We know a little bit of everything, but we actually know nothing, so we have to surround ourselves with people who can support us on this journey and help us learn to deal with this uncertainty.

Horizon scanning is a technique I learned from business, which involves detecting and assessing threats and other potential changes as early as possible. During Covid-19, I had to look globally to do this effectively. Italy was the obvious choice, because they were three weeks ahead of the UK. Listening to Italian school leaders and teachers about the problems they were finding ensured any solution or innovation I created was grounded in some of the problems I could face next. They were telling us about the social and emotional trauma that they and their pupils were experiencing, as well as the sense of isolation and panic created by the lockdowns. They also talked about the scramble to find online options to reach their students and parents, providing an anchor and human connection when there was none.

This gave me a hypothesis that I could take to others. To answer the 'why' question I set out in my framework, I shared my hypothesis before asking:

- Do you think this is the problem?
- Is this the area you need a solution for?

If the answers to both those questions were positive, we moved on to research to find the right tools. From there, we trialled those tools and strategies with a small number of teachers. I monitored their reactions to some of the solutions we found.

Often, we would have five solutions on the table, but I knew I could only afford to progress one. Trying those five very quickly with teachers who understood why they were doing what they were doing, and why they were innovating, allowed me to end up with one solution on the table as quickly as possible.

One such solution was using AI tutors. I had heard from another school that they were using a platform called Century Tech, and I quickly researched, trialled and then purchased the system for everyone. This ensured all our children received instruction and continued to learn, even when our online delivery was disrupted by sickness absence among our teachers. This proved to be a highly effective way to ensure every child learned consistently during this period.

Sowing the seeds for our school

Although I hadn't created this exact problem-solving framework when we started, I certainly had to do my fair share of problem solving at the beginning. You could say this was where I began experimenting with the 'messy journey' of innovation.

Brooklands Farm grew out of fields into one of the UK's largest primary schools – and, as it turned out, we started with a bit of a challenge! Our school sprang into life in 2010, and I had planned to look at the national strategy and develop our curriculum in May of that year. However, then the coalition government came in and changed everything – budget cuts and cuts to services meant that resources disappeared almost overnight. The national strategy changed.

I had to change my approach – and fast. With no dedicated problem-solving tools, I went back to my roots as a nursery headteacher. When I worked in nurseries, I learned my educational theories back to front. All too often people would tell me that my job as a nursery head 'wasn't so important because all we do is play.' At that point, I'd throw all my theory at them. Let's just say that no one would ever tell me that all I did was 'play' again! But this approach proved very useful when I was starting Brooklands.

I knew that if I went back and revisited the best ways to learn, then I would find the best ways to teach. Lev Vygotsky proved particularly useful – he always asked, 'What would that look like for a learner?' Once I'd answered that question, I would ask, 'What would that look like for a teacher?' This allowed me to explore the strategies I could develop to build and grow our school.

This process also gave me a framework that I could use to train anyone who came to work with me. They're all very familiar with Vygotsky now, even if they'd never heard of him before they met me!

My years as a nursery headteacher also made me very good at finding evidence to support my work. This meant I was able to pull in evidence about the techniques for learning and teaching I was recommending for our school, which helped everybody understand our approach (an important part of the first step of my problem-solving framework).

But in the end, we've found being a great teacher comes down to two very simple things:

1. Having knowledge of your curriculum.
2. Getting to know each child and building a relationship.

Really, if you do these two things, everything else falls into place. I did everything I could to simplify the process of sharing our approach and teaching framework. I even recorded short videos designed to demystify what it is to be a teacher. I wanted to build a structure where each member of the team could develop their knowledge and skills to become highly effective.

Bringing everything back to basics has also stopped us from being diverted as a school, even with changes in government. We've had at least three ideas about what the school system 'should look like' from various governments in our 12 years. But when we focus on these basics, we always stay on track. While this framework has proved incredibly valuable, it is not completely rigid.

Freedom within a framework

Within business there is a concept known as 'freedom within a framework'. It's one we've fully embraced at Brooklands. As I'm sure you're aware, if you tell your teachers exactly what you want them to do, 89% of them will go back to their classrooms and do something completely different.

Adopting 'freedom within a framework' helps ensure the quality of teaching throughout the school without dictating exactly how each teacher delivers their lessons. The way I see it, I don't want teachers to do exactly what they're told. I want them to apply their learning to the 30 children sitting in front of them.

Our framework is built on three main beliefs about how children learn best:

1. Children learn holistically.
2. Children and teachers are partners.
3. Children need to own their behaviour and learning journeys.

Our framework

We believe children learn holistically, so the framework focuses on developing their social and emotional disposition to learn the curriculum. In my view, this is just as important as the cognitive curriculum. But unlike the cognitive curriculum, this can be difficult to measure.

We came up with the idea of assigning each year group with a colour and word that celebrated what it was to be a child in that year group. For example, the word for Year 3 is 'balance', because the children in year 3 are unbalanced. Chemicals flood their brains at this age, and this can give them nightmares and mean they can't manage risks. The word 'balance' allows us to explain this to parents more easily. We use stories to explain our approach to each year group, which means that the children are always at the centre of our dialogue.

Similarly, we can use these colours and words to help our children understand how we want them to behave in the learning environment. They provide a golden thread that connects our teachers, children and parents. Our framework is also constructed using wellbeing scales. Children are taught that wellbeing 1 is low, and 5 is high. They are taught to recognise how they are feeling and then plan for how they will self-regulate.

Alongside wellbeing scales, we also teach children learning zone scales. Again, zone 1 is low and reflects when children are unable to learn and adopt meta cognitive skills to ensure they achieve. Meanwhile, zone 5 describes a child who is totally engrossed and will not be diverted from their learning. This strategy has the theory of Vygotsky at its base. Children are taught that the zone of proximal development is 4, and therefore they have self-responsibility to be in learning zone 4. They are also taught that you can only maintain a learning zone 4 for 10 minutes before dipping to a 3. It is vital our children learn how to move from a zone 3 back to a zone 4 to ensure they are in control of their own learning journey.

Similarly, we provide feedback to our teachers based on the percentage of children whose wellbeing is high or whose learning zone is high. Teachers are taught that the observations of wellbeing and learning zones within a lesson allow them to understand if their pitch is correct and whether their lesson is having an impact. Teachers are taught to then adapt their teaching accordingly.

> We introduced a simple five-step framework for implementation to help keep everyone on track:
> 1. Start with the child.
> 2. Use the national curriculum.
> 3. Know your community's needs.
> 4. Weave in evidence while being careful to interpret the evidence and ensure it is based on strong data.
> 5. Provide a consistent, systematic, sequential approach to delivering our curriculum.

A framework for teachers

The frameworks at our school don't stop with our children. I also built a framework for our teachers to support their development as part of my MBA. I was writing my dissertation during the Covid-19 pandemic, and it was focused on teachers. I held space for them and listened to how they wanted to approach the rapid shift from face-to-face teaching to online teaching.

They told me they wanted to take flexible approaches to their CPD, and they did this by coming together as communities of practice that were non-hierarchical. I didn't attend these sessions, but my teachers did ask me to build them a framework so they would know what 'good' looked like. This gave them the structure they needed to plot their journeys to 'good'. Part of that included giving them self-study days.

We allow our teachers to manage their own learning journeys, just like we do with our children. A concept that has worked particularly well – which I stole from Google – is micro moments. These are three-minute videos that, collectively, will add up to a big concept that you want your teachers to learn. The beauty is that most teachers can find three minutes in their days to watch a video. These videos are pushed to their phones, which makes it more likely they will watch them. We're weaving their learning journey into their daily activities.

We have built pathways and rubrics to show what 'good' looks like so each member of the team can map their own journey. All of this information goes on their individual growth plans, which are an important tool for us as a coaching school.

Lessons for your journey

There are three key lessons that have served me well on my journey, and that I believe all headteachers can benefit from embracing.

1. Be realistic

The government and Ofsted are talking a lot about a 'sequential curriculum' at the time of publication. I completely agree with their approach – until you put a child in it. We all know that learning journeys aren't sequential, even if the curriculum is. A child doesn't learn in a straight line – it becomes a squiggle very quickly. So, within education as a whole, we have to stop pretending.

You'll know as well as I do that we cannot fit the whole of the curriculum into the hours we actually have in the context of a recruitment, retention and sickness crisis. But I believe we can borrow an approach from business to help us better prepare and mitigate risks in curriculum delivery.

The approach is to create an issues log where you track lessons learned and highlight anything that may derail the sequence of your curriculum, such as an Anglo-Saxon day being added to the timetable, or someone being off sick. This allows you to be realistic about what you can achieve with your children and gives your teachers tools to be real and honest. Once you are aware of the risks, you can plan.

To be able to do this effectively, we have to come back to the key skill I shared earlier in this chapter: listening. For example, I included Rosenshine's 'Principles of Instruction' in my school improvement plan for three years, and I thought everything was going well – until I asked my teachers whether they were implementing it. I discovered that while 70% of them were, 30% were not.

Having this data was incredibly valuable, as it allowed me to create a plan for the 30% who weren't using Rosenshine and open up dialogues about why they weren't using it. All of this strengthened our school improvement plan.

2. Learn to live with the mistakes

The biggest lesson on your journey from 'good' to 'outstanding', or maintaining 'outstanding', is to learn to live with the mistakes. You're going to make them constantly. People often ask me to teach them how to be a headteacher. I'm happy to provide support, but I tell them straight away that I'm only going to teach them to make mistakes. After spending about a month with me, they often say, 'You make a lot of mistakes, don't you?'

I always reply, 'Yes, I do. But the trick is that I've learned to live with them.' I believe all leaders on the journey to 'outstanding' need to do the same.

Up, up and away

To celebrate our first birthday at Brooklands Farm Primary School, we decided we would do a balloon release. Each balloon would have a label on it to tell people about our school and how proud we are of it. We thought they'd fly all over the country and help lots of people find out about our brand-new school.

The day came. We released 90 balloons into the air, but... I hadn't checked the wind. Ninety bright yellow balloons floated up into the sky, and flew towards the M1, which was just two fields away from us. I started to panic. Then I remembered that after the M1 there was an airfield. Planes would be landing and taking off... and our 90 balloons were travelling straight towards it.

Even though I was all smiles, giving out cake and helping plant a tree, my heart was racing. All I kept thinking was that I could have killed people with my mistake. For the whole afternoon I was listening out for sirens and thinking that if I heard one my career would be over. Luckily our balloons didn't cause any accidents, but it still remains one of my biggest mistakes!

3. Embrace business tools to innovate

I've been a headteacher for 27 years and I have fewer resources now than I have ever had. There is a huge pressure on a leader who is trying to find the right strategy, because if they get it wrong they've got no other way of putting it right. Mistakes are costly, and they weigh heavily on those of us who are trying to find new solutions to improve our school systems. This weight is particularly heavy when national top-down solutions are being given to us.

We have to invest in those solutions, even though we often feel that a different solution is needed. But if we follow a different solution, then we won't pass our Ofsted inspections. So, we don't take those opportunities. They're not safe. And yet we stand up in assemblies, or staff meetings, and work with parents, knowing that at times there is an inability to act to make things better and that hurts. It also deconstructs our credibility, and that is a hard cross to bear.

I think most, if not all, of us agree that the top-down system as it is needs to change. We need a system where educational leaders feel strong, and are able and confident to share and manage change. But changing the system isn't in our power, so what can we do as school leaders? In my experience, the best way to tackle this issue is to develop new ways to think about our role as problem solvers and share the solutions we're finding or the processes we're using to find those solutions.

It's a real shame that within education we often dismiss what business can offer us, by saying things like, 'They don't understand education', or 'They haven't got solutions for us.' Another common statement is, 'We're talking about structure and how schools run financially, or the resources schools have, which is different from how things work in business.' But for all that business is different, there is still a lot we can learn, particularly about how we manage people and go through a process of finding solutions.

Business has a huge role to play in supporting us as school leaders to learn about the tools they're using and the solutions they are finding. Covid-19 was just the start. AI and what that will do to the school system and learning in general is the next big thing that's coming over the hill for those of us in schools. This is going to affect businesses too.

Yet we're still not liaising with businesses as much as we could. We're still not talking to business leaders, and we haven't linked school leaders and business leaders together to discuss solutions. I'd love this to change. I want headteachers to feel empowered to ask business leaders what they're doing, what tools they're using and how they're ensuring their staff learn about the changes they need to make in the face of all this new technology.

For all that studying for my MBA during the Covid-19 pandemic was challenging, it gave me an incredible opportunity to identify similarities between schools and businesses, and learn what tools and strategies the education system could adopt from the business world. We were all facing the same problems and having to adapt rapidly to the changing landscape.

My MBA opened up a new way of thinking and provided me with new tools to innovate and solve the problems that my learning community was facing. My strength now lies in always looking to business for solutions. I'm not afraid to horizon scan across both the business and education sectors. However, the challenges of recruitment and the pace of change with limited resources have made any mistakes I do make more critical and costly.

This is why the problem-solving framework I shared with you earlier is crucial, as it minimises the risk of my mistakes. I believe the opportunities lie within the networks I choose to collaborate with – you could find such opportunities in your networks too. Building on the processes, systems and strategies we have in schools is more important now than ever.

Change is on the horizon

Covid-19 was the first major disruptor I had come across as a school leader, but there are more coming. AI is at our heels. Climate change is going to have a massive impact on the solutions that leaders are going to have to find.

For example, in the last three years we have taught in classrooms that are 40°C. This does not make sense. But unless we start to talk about the things we are facing and have been facing over the last three years, we are not going to be able to share and develop strategies that allow us to use the resources that we have well. I am concerned that if school leaders aren't celebrated and innovation isn't shared, then they sit in isolation and their mental health will worsen.

I would like every school leader to share their stories of innovation. They are doing it day in and day out, with the little tweaks that they're making. We need to share our innovation journeys to demystify the process of problem solving and help others learn how leaders in schools actually problem solve.

By demystifying it, we could make it more acceptable for others to talk about it so we can all learn from each other. I want every headteacher to be in a strong network where they are able to collaborate, share innovation and discuss how a solution is taken from theory or evidence and then put into practice.

The ability to move from strategic to operational can be quite a journey for a leader. Having peers to talk to about that can only be beneficial. The collaborations and networks that headteachers need to join are ones that are open and honest and where those involved truly want collaboration in their hearts. These people don't see innovation as a competition or one-upmanship on the solutions that they're finding.

As school leaders we balance a lot of complexity. We are public servants, and as such we have top-down frameworks that we have to exist within. These have to be balanced with a bottom-up approach that we use within our schools.

I believe we need to talk about this complexity more explicitly so we can share the pressures of being a public servant who has to hold up the national understanding about how teachers and children learn, while also facing our communities' needs.

Balancing the bottom-up approach we use day to day with sitting in a top-down structure can lead to frustration. Often this means school leaders haven't got the energy to find the solutions and the innovations that are really needed in a bottom-up system. This is another example of why listening to and collaborating with others is so important – it can help all of us find solutions and show us that we're not alone in this struggle.

Change is coming, whether we like it or not. Within education, we are all innovators – perhaps more than we realise. We have the collective strength and knowledge to tackle these changes head-on for the good of our children, teachers, parents and wider communities. But I believe we can only do this if we support one another on our journeys and accept support from outside the education arena.

TOP TIPS

- ★ Learn to listen and hold space for others so you can identify the challenges facing your teachers and pupils. Use the information you gather from listening more deeply to help lay the foundations for sustainable solutions.
- ★ Create a network of collaborators both inside and outside of your school. Share ideas and receive feedback from them before you implement any major changes. Use the problem-solving framework to help you navigate this process.
- ★ Look to the world of business for innovations you can bring into your school and encourage others in your school to embrace a culture of innovation and change.

Chapter 6:
Using inspections as catalysts – Beth Dyer

Meet Beth...

Beth Dyer is the headteacher at Nine Acres Primary School on the Isle of Wight. Her school has a high number of pupils from disadvantaged backgrounds, so they place particular focus on helping children develop the skills and resilience they'll need to progress throughout their lives. The school was judged as 'outstanding' in July 2024, the first 'outstanding' school on the Isle of Wight since 2011.

About Nine Acres Primary School

	School	National Average
Pupils with a SEND Education, Health and Care Plan	3.3%	2.5%
Pupils with SEND support	14.9%	13.5%
Pupils whose first language is not English	6.3%	22.0%
Pupils eligible for free school meals at any time during the past six years	29.1%	25.9%

> There's no getting away from the fact that the context of our school is significant deprivation, and that we have many disadvantaged and vulnerable pupils. As a school we're on a real mission, because we know these children can't get out of the poverty trap they're stuck in unless they have a fundamental education. Doing nice things with them, like creating beautiful art or going to see an orchestra, won't change that fact.
>
> As a school, we track every intervention we make, assess whether it's working and change it if necessary. Our children are already vulnerable, and their life chances have already been limited, so we want to be accountable for helping to change that.
>
> But we're under no illusions that we can do everything. You'll know as well as I do that we can't remove all the barriers our children face, because many of them go far beyond the school gate. What we can do is help our children develop the skills and resilience they need to get themselves over their barriers. As a primary school, we see our role as laying strong foundations on which our children can build as they move into secondary school and beyond. What I'm going to share with you in this chapter is how we have made use of Ofsted as a catalyst for improvement.

Leaning into accountability

There are systems of accountability in all professions, whether they are to customers, patients, staff, parents, children or, in fact, to ourselves. Transparent accountability allows us to keep striving for excellence, generating new ideas and becoming innovative. This is not about perfection; perfection does not lead to growth. It's about celebrating what has been achieved and using this knowledge to look beyond.

When everyone is, and wants to be, responsible for their actions and their results, a school culture can become exceptional. It's like the holy grail we all strive for – and there have been some incredible examples shared already in this book with suggestions as to how to move the needle in this area. Accountability is inherent in the teaching profession. Without an accountability system, assessing the quality of education children receive, which enables them to succeed in today's world, would be challenging for all of us.

As a head yourself, you'll be all too aware of the many systems of accountability present within education, be they from the local authority, peer-to-peer, school-led, national outcomes or through the parent community. And, of course, Ofsted.

Ofsted is a contentious issue. On the one hand, I don't think any of us mind the accountability that Ofsted offers. Most of us in the teaching profession welcome areas for improvement being highlighted. But the difficulty with the Ofsted regime, I believe, is that it's done *to* schools, not done *with* schools.

A point-in-time judgement

I deliberately use the word 'judgement' here, rather than evaluated, reflected upon or discussed, because that is what Ofsted does – it judges you and your school in just two days. There's no room within that framework to help develop us as schools.

As headteachers, we welcome accountability. But the point of accountability is to learn and grow, and as we all know, learning from an inspection sometimes feels like an impossible task. In addition to feeling like inspections are being done *to* us, the judgements we receive as a result are based on a specific point in time, rather than capturing the full picture.

It seems unfair that in some instances the report does not capture the true essence of a school. Paul even told us in chapter 4 about how he fought an Ofsted assessment he didn't agree with – and good for him! But we don't necessarily have the time (or want to spend it) arguing semantics with Ofsted inspectors. A school context is not an excuse for poor performance, as Helen explained in chapter 3, but it does change the processes and priorities that school leaders put in place. I'm willing to bet that if we compared my processes and priorities to yours, they would be different – and rightly so – but the challenges and opportunities at your school are also likely to be different from those at mine.

This is why I believe, and I'm sure you'll agree, the one-size-fits-all framework does not work and does not provide a school with the opportunity to learn, build and innovate for their community, as Maxine rightly points out in chapter 5. Instead, schools and leaders are often held to ransom for improvement, causing distress and disharmony. No school leader steps into the profession wanting their school to fail.

This means that we find ourselves held to account by a generic framework written by inspectors who do not know our school, our context, our challenges or our uniqueness. They do not stand at the school gate with us every day. This can feel like you are going to have to play the game or tick the box to pass a test. But who is this for?

When we're handed an Ofsted report for our school, it can be all too easy to set about making the recommended improvements. We want to deliver the best for our children, and surely following this guidance will deliver that… However, at each point we must ask, 'Does this change the lives of our children in schools?' Sometimes what's being suggested may not. As heads, we have the challenging role of taking this external accountability process, making it work for us and owning it. We have to find a way to look beyond the tick list and redefine inspections as opportunities for professional development and therefore school improvement.

Finding opportunities for growth

How can we take this process and use it to help us grow and strengthen the knowledge and skills of our profession? What I've learned through asking this question at my school is that there is more we can control than we perhaps realise. But equally, there are some variables outside our control, and we have to be able to let go of those so we can control the controllables.

When schools can be judged as 'good' or even 'outstanding' by Ofsted, it's a cause for celebration. However, is that sufficient? It's a hard question to ask yourself when you feel the elation of receiving a 'good' or 'outstanding' Ofsted rating at your school. But what I've realised is that this point-in-time judgement is simply recognition that our school's processes work and the school understands itself well. However, we can't let this stop us striving for more.

Instead, we have to find a way to use this judgement to motivate us to strengthen, share and deepen our processes and continue growing. We embrace accountability because we desire more for our children, who will lead our future society.

In my experience, redefining the inspection process allows schools to continuously enhance the educational offer and provide a positive, safe and conducive atmosphere for all stakeholders. This takes bravery and positivity, especially when the Ofsted accountability framework is flawed in so many ways. However, we also have to acknowledge the value that Ofsted brings by giving us a nationally consistent framework in which to work.

What Ofsted provides is a consistent way in which to hold ourselves to account for our children in a way that gives us a national comparison. This means the children at my school can stand up next to the children at any other school in the country and are prepared for the next stages of their journey. Given the level of deprivation our children have, we could lose sight of the national level that their peers will be achieving – and we can't do that if we want them to have the best chance in life. The way I think of this is that every child who joins Nine Acres in Reception is going to leave in seven years, so we need to teach them what they need to go beyond us, wherever that may be.

What we've realised is that the opportunities for growth from Ofsted don't come from the inspections and judgements themselves, but from taking the inspection regime Ofsted uses and making it work for us and our children.

This means looking beyond the inspection itself and at what Ofsted ultimately wants to achieve: the best possible education for children across the country. We've used this to help develop our staff as curriculum leaders who are asking the right questions, interrogating the data, going into classrooms and evaluating our curriculum over time. Time is the key – unlike a snap two-day inspection, this gives all of us an opportunity to reflect and question what we're doing. We can ask, 'These children aren't getting where they need to, why is that?' We can unpick this to work out what we need to do and how we can do that sustainably over time.

Are you sitting comfortably...

At the beginning of this chapter, I talked about the barriers our children face. One that is particularly acute among our pupils is reading – and more specifically, many children not having regular reading time with their parents at home. We know that a lot of the parents in our community have a lot going on and often have multiple children, so we quickly realised that nagging them to do more reading time just wasn't going to work. We changed our approach.

We put the challenge back to our children by asking them to think about when they could find time in their school day to read. We encourage our children to read for pleasure during lunchtime or break time. They know that if they want to stay behind after school for 10-15 minutes to do some reading they can. They also know that if they finish an activity in class early they can ask to use the remainder of that time to catch up on their reading and that this will be welcomed. As well as encouraging them to read more, we've also taught them that they don't have to rely on adults to do that activity.

The other way in which we've tackled this challenge is to focus our resources on our children to help improve their reading levels. Every day at 2.45pm, all our support staff go to Year 1 and each child gets to sit and read to an adult at the end of their school day. This will happen for six weeks, and then the support staff will rotate and go to early years and then to Year 2. This is just one example of how we've deployed our resources a bit differently.

Rather than our support staff running around making sure everyone has got their coat or closed their locker at the end of the school day, they're using that time to help the younger children advance their reading. What's fantastic is that everyone in the school gets behind this and improving reading has become embedded at every level.

We also make sure that all our curriculum leaders, including those in subjects like PE, RE and art, have reading in their action plan for our children who are reading below age-related expectations and are identified as the lowest 20% of our readers. That means we're always looking at how we can make sure reading isn't a barrier for those children in those subjects – which they otherwise may well excel at – while ensuring that reading infiltrates every part of the curriculum.

The best school improvement – one that is truly impactful and embedded – is when there is a clear understanding of why things may need to improve or be developed further and how this can be achieved in context. Redefining the school inspection system in our minds and viewing it as a supportive side-by-side process allows for this.

When we learn from one another, observe successful practices in action and trust in their effectiveness, our own improvement journey and the school system are more likely to succeed. I'm sure that's one of the reasons you're reading this book.

Individual schools may want to redefine what the inspection process looks like, what it feels like, what it provides us with. However, the current framework does not allow such flexibility. What we can do is control how the inspection process affects us and find ways to make it work for both us as individuals and as schools. As we move forward as educators, it is vital we hold on to our moral compass – we know our schools and our community well. Redefining this inspection process in our minds creates a climate for healthy challenge and healthy development, while putting every child at the heart of the process.

Going beyond compliance

I think many of us have found that it's all too easy to get caught up in the paperwork when preparing for inspections. I know I've certainly got hung up on the template of what we need in our Ofsted folder in the past. We all know it's important that statutory requirements and compliance are in place to keep children safe, and we welcome it. But that doesn't mean the Ofsted process is flawless – as I'm sure most of us would agree, it's far from perfect!

We could easily spend hours debating the merits of Ofsted, but while we may enjoy a good vent, it won't help us move ourselves or our schools forward. Instead, we can work out how to take the Ofsted process and embed it into the school culture with fairness, compassion and a sense of reality. I know this can be difficult in a system that can at times feel unfair, but I've found that reframing it in this way is what can drive the school improvement agenda.

Teachers are creative people – they innovate, and they go into the profession to change lives. I know that's why I entered education.

A process aligned to the school context with clear outcomes allows teachers to see their impact. At Nine Acres, we've taken a pragmatic approach to engaging with redefining the inspection process. This has involved adapting the processes to be more efficient, effective and aligned to the needs of the school context.

That sounds simple enough, but the 'how' is a bit trickier. We've achieved this by making sure we all understand what needs to be done and why, rather than focusing on the simplicity of compliance and clarity.

Taking a deep dive

I'm sure you're familiar with the Ofsted 'deep dive' process. When it launched, there was (and still is) a lot of noise around it. There are a lot of online articles telling you what it involves, then there are consultants who you can pay to come into your school and talk you through a deep dive, but as a school we were still left wondering what it actually looked like as a process – so we went back to the source.

We only took what was in the Ofsted briefing and watched the videos about what a deep dive is on the Ofsted YouTube channel. This was a hugely valuable exercise for me personally, because I realised I had got caught up in the 'commercial' (tick-box) aspects of the inspection rather than remembering why we have these inspections in the first place, namely to deliver a better standard of education for our children. The document we found particularly helpful was the Ofsted inspection framework, which sets out the deep dive process in great detail.

As a school, we took that process and worked through it with our curriculum leaders. At Nine Acres, we don't teach by topic or theme – we teach subjects in their own right, and we found this process incredibly valuable because it allowed us to look at each subject in its entirety as it's taught to pupils of all ages. Some of the questions we asked ourselves were:

- Is each subject taught to the same standard across different classes?
- Are SEND children getting the same deal?
- Are the children who are really good at that subject being challenged enough?

- What does this look like as a whole subject for a child, from Reception to Year 6?
- What does that subject look like as a journey? For example, if a child wanted to study geography at GCSE or A-level, how would our geography lessons feed into that ambition?

We took this Ofsted process and made it work for us, and in doing so we gained really great insights and had very deep and meaningful conversations between our teachers. We realised that if we weren't deliberate and purposeful in how we taught each subject at each level, we may not be giving our children the ambition and passion to study certain subjects at a higher level.

Carrying out this deep dive process made us realise that in some subjects we had serious work to do. We realised that certain subjects didn't have the integrity we thought they did – the children weren't remembering what they learned and weren't enjoying it either. They weren't developing the vocabulary to take it further and the level of learning wasn't high enough. When we did this for our history and geography curriculum, we all had a moment of realisation when we knew we needed to do something different.

As a result of carrying out this deep dive exercise, we completely revamped our history and geography curriculum. When we initially wrote our history and geography curriculum, we thought it was good, and we thought it aligned with our vision, although I'm sure we would have realised it wasn't working further down the line. However, without having done the deep dive and really examining the curriculum at every level, we would likely have made changes based on our gut feeling, or perhaps blamed a teacher in a particular year group. Instead, we used the Ofsted process as an accountability exercise for ourselves to ensure we were delivering really high-quality subjects to our children.

Together, we challenged ourselves. We developed our language of learning so it became consistent between leaders and we all knew what was being said. We reviewed our monitoring and evaluation cycles at all points, problem solving together – and, of course, over time we celebrated those wins.

This was not a top-down accountability process. This was a side-by-side process we used as a team and that we were all responsible for. In doing so, we redefined the inspection process from being one that passed judgement on us to one that supported but also challenged our thinking.

As a result of this work, the curriculum already looked better than it did the term before. There was more work in books, teachers were enjoying teaching, pupils' progress in books was evident and children talked about their subject with enthusiasm and knowledge. This was okay – it was certainly better than it was. We could have ticked the box of 'achieved "outstanding", rapid progress is evident'. But was it good enough?

We didn't make a point-in-time judgement – we knew that tomorrow would bring different challenges, new children would join the school along with new staff and some of our children would forget their key knowledge. By redefining and using the deep dive process, our leaders used that accountability to measure successes and strive for more.

What we created was a continuous improvement strategy that meant we had the highest expectations that no child, no group of children, no staff member was left falling behind. Our school culture changed, and our beliefs changed. All of a sudden, we could see what was possible.

Preparing for inspections

I always think preparing for an inspection is like preparing for a special event where you want everyone to see what success looks like in your school. I'm sure I'm not alone in this. But thinking of it as a special event where we're going to showcase our school makes it feel exciting rather than terrifying.

Imagine you are holding an art exhibition for the community. You learn the knowledge and skills needed to create your masterpiece. You practise the skill, you gather your resources, you refine your creation, reflect, and then consider the most effective way to present your masterpiece. Then you welcome people in to see your work.

You feel confident, excited and ready to explain your choice of design and your reasons why. You own the work, and no matter what others think of your masterpiece you are proud of it, because you have worked so hard in getting it to this point. You have prepared.

Imagine not preparing. How would you feel?

If I hadn't fully prepared for an event like this, I know I'd be more nervous than excited. I'd be worried about what I'd say and how my work would come across. I may even feel like I'd done just enough, rather than given my best. None of us want to feel like that – especially when we're presenting our schools. However, the stress of school inspections can make it feel this way.

I don't need to tell you how important preparation is to ensure our schools demonstrate their commitment to their provision and show they're compliant with statutory regulations. However, when we're caught up in the stress of preparation for inspection, it can sometimes be easy – even just momentarily – to lose sight of why we're really here. We want to provide the best learning environment for our children and a workplace that supports our staff and leaders to do their best work – I don't know about you, but I find sometimes it's helpful to have this reminder, because it brings me back to what's really important.

The idea of preparing is not about painting a perfect picture – authenticity is the real key. When a school presents itself with clear rationales and clear awareness of development, this demonstrates true substantive educational improvement. Schools that try to present a perfect image may not prioritise the children at the heart of their actions; often that's an unintentional consequence of the way in which we approach inspections – with fear and dread in our hearts, instead of pride.

As heads, we'd all love to give our team time to feel prepared for these inspections. We want them to have the chance to reflect, refine and practise – but in a busy school environment, how on earth do you manage that?

We have found coaching to be a really effective tool, especially for our middle leaders. Again, we took inspiration from Ofsted, but we weren't coaching our team to answer questions at an Ofsted inspection – we were coaching them to become more forensic in their ambitions and action plans.

The way we did this was to look at the Ofsted handbook to find the questions that middle leaders would be asked during an inspection. We took those questions and used them to form the basis of our coaching, so we could help each person not only to speak passionately about their subject, but also to be able to identify and articulate weaknesses in that area.

We made sure we asked questions that went beyond the subject itself. Some examples of our coaching questions include:

- What are behaviours and attitudes like in your subject?
- What does it look like for a child to be safe in your subject?
- How is personal development included in your subject?

These are tough questions, but by making them part of a coaching conversation, my passionate, enthusiastic leaders got fired up and became really clear about what their subjects needed to deliver beyond what was going on in the curriculum. This helped them to set much clearer and more valuable priorities for their subjects too.

Now, instead of a priority being, 'I must book that trip to Winchester science museum', it became, 'I must get the vocabulary sorted in Year 5 for science because that's the difference between those children being able to progress in this subject and not.' This process has also led to us introducing pre-teaching for certain subjects – such as design and technology – to make sure all our children have the knowledge they need at each stage of their education to progress further in that subject.

As well as leading to better outcomes for our children, this meant that when the inspection did happen, our teachers could articulate how personal development was used in history teaching, or how something from our PSHE curriculum fed into our science curriculum.

The value of self-assessment

Schools can use the process of preparing for inspections as a catalyst for improvement by approaching it as holistic self-assessment rather than aiming to simply meet narrow inspection criteria. We can conduct a thorough self-assessment to identify areas that need improvement, not just those outlined in the inspection criteria. I've found that this has worked wonders for Nine Acres.

We've found that the key to achieving this is to involve teachers, pupils, parents and other stakeholders in that preparation process, as their insights contribute their diverse perspectives and foster a sense of shared responsibility for that improvement. Our school leadership team can then establish realistic and achievable improvement goals that are based not only on the inspection criteria, but more importantly on internal assessments.

This approach ensures the goals we set align with our school's unique context and challenges. By integrating inspection preparation into a broader strategy for continuous improvement, we can transform the process from a compliance-driven task into a dynamic force that positively shapes the educational experience for everybody involved.

Use what you've got

One thing we found very comforting was using the Ofsted accountability system that's already in place. We didn't have to come up with our own set of measures for accountability – we were able to shape and amend the one that already exists and that all of us are already measured against. This made it much easier to not only start embedding this process in our school, but also ensure we were measuring up against national standards too.

Preparation for an Ofsted inspection should not just take place in the inspection window either. I'm sure that's the dream for all of us – to not have a last-minute scramble to get ready. Although, of course there will always be those last-minute paperwork trails – who will be doing what on the day – and a wish for more time. However, in the best schools, when the call comes there is a sense of, 'Finally, let's go for it!' This is because these schools are always ready.

You've heard from several heads in this book who reached a point of not only being ready for Ofsted, but being impatient for the inspectors to come! If that's where you'd like your school to get to, my advice is to focus on embedding an ethos of continuous improvement into your school culture that uses the framework and leans into the positive impact it can have.

There is no denying that the feedback from Ofsted inspections can feel demoralising at times, especially when it is very critical. Even though we all know that a school culture that is outward looking and welcomes feedback from all stakeholders is ultimately one that is always prepared for an inspection of any kind, and that exceptional leaders take feedback, whether it is good or bad, and do something with it, this is often easier said than done. Turning any feedback, but particularly negative, into action to create, develop and enhance a school can seem like an uphill battle. The good news is that often all that's required is a mindset shift to help us learn from inspections, rather than feel demoralised by them.

When we can take the feedback from inspections as learning points, we can be confident something will change for the better. It may take time, and success may not be linear, but as educators this is what we do every day with the children we teach. We help them take small steps towards improvement.

Empowering subject leaders through reflective practice

As part of our three-year development plan at Nine Acres, we chose the development point that all leaders should use assessment and monitoring of their subject to identify and plan proactively to close gaps in knowledge, understanding and skills from the baseline measure.

We invited an independent consultant to work alongside our subject leaders, supporting them to be able to talk about their subject and in turn develop their strategic leadership for their area. It shaped their thinking, their clarity and in turn their actions and next steps. This had an impact on what was happening in classrooms and as a result children were receiving a better curriculum entitlement.

On the morning that we received the call from Ofsted to tell us they were on their way, there was a sense of calm, confidence and determination because those subject leaders knew their subject. They knew the good parts and they also knew the parts that still needed development. They walked into the inspection and took control. They led the inspection.

They told the inspector what he needed to know because that was normal in our school. It was normal to lay out the books and look at a thread of learning. It was normal to point out the impact of team teaching. It was normal to enter into professional discussion that challenged our thinking.

As a result, our Ofsted inspection report left us with no areas for improvement. This was not because we were perfect. It was because it was clear we knew our school well and we knew what our next steps were.

Inspections as a catalyst for learning and improvement

Continuous improvement is part of school life, and I've found it incredibly useful to reframe inspections as just another opportunity for continuous improvement. Rather than being a big, scary process, these inspections are an opportunity to gather valuable feedback and insights into the strengths and weaknesses of our educational offer. When I started thinking of inspections in this way, I found it liberating.

By embracing and implementing the lessons learned from each inspection, I know we can enhance teaching methods, curriculum design and overall educational provision. This ongoing learning process ensures our school evolves and adapts to better meet the needs of our pupils, creating a dynamic and effective learning environment.

I know it may be hard, but we have to try to take the emotion out of the inspection process to be able to have these open and honest conversations, engage with feedback, extract actionable insights and prioritise activity. This process can be a great catalyst to share, talk and challenge within your team. I've found it helpful to keep coming back to why we're doing this – to support our children and give them the skills and knowledge they need to overcome the barriers they face throughout their lives, not just in the seven years they're with us.

We have to keep reminding ourselves that this feedback has come from somewhere, even if it's challenging. Our job is to find where it's come from and to unpick it. But as a team, don't forget to stop and celebrate what you have succeeded in. There are many positives; hold on to these. Think about what you can change, but only in the context of your school. Always consider the impact of every action you take – if it changes the course of just one child for the better, then surely it's worth it.

Learning from feedback

Our school is among the bottom 10% of schools for deprivation nationally. In our recent Ofsted inspection, we were challenged about the expectations we held for our parent community. We explained to the inspector about our traditional parents' evenings, occasional reading mornings, crafting mornings, and the workshops we'd offered for parents to join their child in maths but that few had attended.

This prompted us to reflect on how we could become more welcoming to our parent community and involve them more in their children's educational journey. We realised that we had been so focused on the experiences and opportunities for our children that we had not extended our outreach to their parents.

Although we were doing a great job at empowering our pupils, we had fallen into the trap of not empowering our parent community to support their child's educational journey, regardless of their own experiences with schools. If it hadn't been for the inspector's comment, we may not have taken the time to reflect on this aspect, as our mindset was fixed on doing everything for the children.

This led us to open up more as a school, and even if only two parents attended a workshop or activity, we considered it a success and a foundation for further growth.

As a school leader, I have worked in schools labelled with special measures. At this point, you feel the to-do list is endless – there's no money, no time, and what you thought was embedded suddenly unravels. If you're in that place now, please don't lose heart. This is only a moment in time.

The children, the staff and the community need you, so take time to refresh yourself and reinvigorate yourself by visiting other schools and talking to other like-minded leaders. No one school is alone, and no leader is alone in this journey. The key to overcoming these challenges is to embrace them as a catalyst for growth and find other people to support you on your journey.

> **TOP TIPS**
>
> ★ Redefine the inspection process by asking yourself and your team, 'Would implementing this feedback change the lives of the children in our school for the better?' Every time you answer 'yes' to that question, you enhance the value of the inspection.
> ★ Follow the Ofsted deep dive process as a team to challenge and interrogate your curriculum to find areas for improvement.
> ★ Turn the process of preparing for an inspection into a holistic, ongoing self-assessment of your school and look beyond the inspection criteria to find areas where you could improve.

Chapter 7:
Cultivating a high-performing team – Paula Philips

Meet Paula...

Paula Philips is the headteacher at East Wichel Community Primary School & Nursery in Swindon, an area that has received some bad press for the quality of its education offering. The government even named it as an education 'cold spot' in its levelling up agenda. However, Paula and her team are striving to change the perception that education in Swindon is universally poor. Not only does Paula's school deliver outstanding education, but it does so in a way that supports staff health, wellbeing and happiness.

About East Wichel Community Primary School & Nursery

	School	National average
Pupils with a SEND Education, Health and Care Plan	1.7%	2.5%
Pupils with SEND support	13.1%	13.5%
Pupils whose first language is not English	33.4%	22.0%
Pupils eligible for free school meals at any time during the past six years	14.2%	25.9%

> Growing up, I was a free school meals child. My mum was one of eight children. She left school early to care for her younger siblings, and as a result has literacy difficulties. Despite these difficulties, she gave me a really strong work ethic, instilled good values in me and she listened to me read every day. This has given me a lifelong love of reading.
>
> In fact, I love reading so much that when I was 11 I accidentally got locked in the local public library one summer's evening because I was so engrossed reading *Anne of Green Gables* (incidentally, she was one of my first teacher heroes). I've wanted to be a teacher for as long as I can remember. I would line my dolls up for registration – it was all I thought and dreamed about. I was very fortunate to have great teachers at my school who believed in me and taught me well.
>
> But several years into teaching, I felt unhealthy. I wasn't taking care of myself, and I knew this needed to change. I love my job and know that my work – and all of our work – matters. We're the profession that holds the future of society in its hands. We have a huge influence and ability to impact the world. But putting that before my own needs was killing me. I was aware I needed a new approach.
>
> I turned to books to help me develop myself. Self-development has been pivotal on my journey, and as I'll share in this chapter, I believe learning underpins a high-performing team.

A crisis crossroads

I started as the headteacher at East Wichel in January 2019. Just over a year later, and you all know what happened: the Covid-19 pandemic hit. My stress hit new levels. For all we knew in March 2020, this could have been the beginning of the end of the world.

Everything I loved about my role and gave me satisfaction, joy and pleasure in my work was stripped away. I was left writing 54-page risk assessments in fear, with very little support, unrealistic expectations and stressful deadlines, facing a fragmented, resentful and sometimes angry community. I almost broke.

I stood at a crossroads, both personally and professionally. I felt I had three choices:

1. I could walk away.
2. I could carry on as I was, becoming more miserable, bitter and twisted in every way and end up hating my life.
3. I could reframe how I was viewing the situation and change my mindset.

I knew I couldn't change the circumstances, but I realised I could change my thoughts. I believed I could figure things out, so I chose option number three, and in doing so my self-development process was significantly accelerated.

I realised no one was coming to save us. The only way we could make the system truly better for everyone was from the inside. So I turned back to my first love: reading. I read everything I could get my hands on. I read books about building powerful teams, managing stress, wellbeing, mindfulness, productivity, how to communicate well and even customer service.

I knew that if I could develop myself, I could develop my team. After all, human beings have done the most incredible things as teams – we've crossed oceans and travelled to the moon. We are capable of so much.

Even without the Covid-19 pandemic in the mix, what we do in schools is becoming increasingly complex and diverse. It can be challenging to navigate your way through all the noise and nonsense at times. As headteachers, we're running incredibly complicated human organisations, often with minimal funding, less than optimal staffing levels, poor resourcing and enormous external pressures, demands, updates and accountability.

What we do is not easy, and creating a truly exceptional culture within our schools can be a challenge. This challenge is too much for any one individual, and the only way to get there is by building a high-performing team.

> 'Never doubt that a small group of thoughtful, committed citizens can change the world: indeed, it's the only thing that ever has.'
>
> **Margaret Mead, anthropologist**

What is a high-performing team?

Before I talk about what a high-performing team is, I want to challenge six common beliefs and tell you what I think it's *not*:

1. It's not about ticking boxes to get the 'outstanding badge', although I would argue you cannot really fail to get to 'outstanding' with a compelling vision and a truly high-performing team.
2. It's not about the individual strengths and skills within your existing team, but rather the relationships, collaboration and synergy between those individuals.
3. It's not about perfection. There are occasions when good enough really is just that. It's the relentless, shared commitment to focusing on those needle movers that drive successful change and progress within any organisation.
4. It's not about being the same as any other team, or indeed any other school. Tapping into your wonderful uniqueness as a team is the key to unlocking potential and removing any perceived glass ceilings.
5. It's not about you or your team working yourselves to death. The fact is that we do our very best when we feel at our very best. So it is essential that some kind of harmony is reached. Finding satisfaction, joy and balance within our work and lives is absolutely critical.
6. Finally, it's not a race. Nothing truly great in life is ever achieved without hard work and a great deal of time. Hold your ground if anyone tries to tell you differently. Building high-performing teams takes trust, tenacity and time.

So, if that's what a high-performing team isn't, then what is it?

A high-performing team is a group of people with diverse skills who work in an almost flow-like, relentless state towards a shared goal. It is a set of living relationships built from a place of psychological safety, where everyone is free to troubleshoot, innovate, make decisions and take risks in line with the shared vision for the organisation.

This team is always seeking to learn, grow and find solutions. It works within the realms of what-ifs and what could be possible, and is not constrained by perceived hierarchies, what has happened before or unnecessary bureaucracies, processes and systems.

A high-performing team is therefore not something you are, but rather the things that you do. Such a team cultivates a shared awareness and ownership of where we are now, the direction of travel, where we want to go next, the problems being faced and how we could get there. In short, a high-performing team adds up to be greater than the sum of its individual parts.

As the headteacher, I'm like the sat-nav on this journey. Our destination is our vision, which we learned from Sonia has to be fiercely ambitious, meaningful and so compelling that it inspires everyone around us to want to be part of it. On that journey, it is the tenacity, creativity and innovation of a high-performing team that is an absolute game-changer for building something that is truly exceptional. None of us can do this alone.

But my role isn't only about focusing everyone on what needs to be done. I also remind them of all the teeny-tiny wins along the way. Celebrating the small wins generates momentum, which drives motivation. A little like one of those old-fashioned roundabouts I played on as a child, in that once you set the roundabout in motion, it begins to feel easier and almost appears to run itself.

Meeting challenges with high performance

The work we do in schools is highly complex, multifaceted and diverse. It can feel impossible at times, and yet we get it done. In most schools it's done exceptionally well, even in the face of significant challenges. If there's one thing that I learned from Covid-19, it's this: get a group of school staff together in one room – socially distanced, of course – and there is very little those people cannot achieve together.

As you well know, we face challenges such as funding, less than optimal staffing levels, poor resources, unsuitable buildings, increasing demands on behaviour and increasing need, especially in this post-Covid-19 world. Then there are the internal and external pressures, demands, updates and accountability as well.

How do we balance all of these challenges, plus the significant workload, and build a high-performing team, while also remembering to be a human being, a mum, a dad, a daughter, a son or a significant other, enjoying this rich and full human experience?

I believe the answer lies in schools supporting schools, learning from each other and growing together. It is by strengthening the system from within and doing so together in a relentless and holistic way that we will solve the challenges we're facing. This is also how we can build high-performing teams and exceptional, happy schools.

Going far, together

It is often said that if you want to go fast, go alone; if you want to go far, go together. While you can create short-term change without a high-performing team, it won't last. Remember that people support what *they* create.

I once knew a headteacher who took on a good school that was in danger of being downgraded. Ofsted was imminent; the exiting headteacher warned the new head that the inspection could go either way. Unfortunately, things were not quite how the new head would have wanted them to be.

Time was of the essence, and the pressure on the team, head and the whole leadership structure was huge. The school was in quite a mess. Change needed to happen, and it needed to happen fast. This shaped and influenced the way the head worked. They put in the work themselves and did a great job. They were great for the whole school community and took the pressure off considerably.

For the team, however, this was a hollow victory. It hadn't been a team effort, but a top-down one. Rather than the change being done *with* them, it had been done *to* them. In the end, they were stressed, overworked, demoralised and disempowered. They'd had no say or ownership in the decisions made, and they were unclear of the vision and the 'why'.

> Not long after, that headteacher moved on, and things reverted back to exactly how they were previously. As the team had had no part in creating the change, they weren't able to sustain it. To sustain and grow something truly exceptional in the long term, we need to build a high-performing team to come with us on the journey. Otherwise, we won't be able to innovate, grow, change and sustain that change.

Six steps for high performance

At East Wichel, we have created a simplified six-step process to create a framework for high performance. These steps are:

1. Look after yourself like it's your job.
2. Find something meaningful.
3. Clarify your core drivers.
4. Eliminate wherever you can.
5. Seek efficiency.
6. Build systems.

1. Look after yourself like it's your job

As a headteacher or part of the senior leadership team, everything starts with you. As you'll be aware, you set the tone for your school culture, and everyone learns from you. This is why we have to spend time figuring out who we want to be as leaders and what tone we want to set.

I have expended energy in the past wishing it was easier, but I've learned it's better to put our energy and focus on building the strongest, healthiest, happiest, most capable versions of ourselves. I want to help you become the person who can handle anything that comes your way and find joy in each day. I promise this also makes leading a school *feel* easier.

I found it helpful to begin my journey down this path by thinking about the kind of leader I would want to work for. The following questions helped me with this process:

- How would they hold themselves?

- How would they interact with others in the best *and* in the worst of times?
- How would they make others feel?
- What would you want them to do?
- What would you want them to say?

Once you've spent time visualising that leader, you can start showing up as the best version of yourself by embodying those traits and behaviours. I've found the following four approaches particularly helpful when becoming the best version of myself. Perhaps they can help you too!

Make time to be inspired

As leaders, one of our main roles is to inspire, lift and empower others. This means we have to top up our own tanks. This may involve reading a book, listening to a podcast, networking with other schools and headteachers, going to conferences or travelling.

I've also found it useful to think about my vision and goals as a leader – and to stick reminders of these everywhere – because this helps me get excited about things and keeps me motivated. Motivation increases satisfaction, fulfils our sense of purpose and feeds into greater happiness and wellbeing.

Work on your physical health

We are biological beings, and everything is interconnected. Our health is the gift on which everything else is built. What we do requires an inordinate amount of energy, enthusiasm and positivity.

I like to think of my body as an elite racehorse, and I treat it accordingly. You wouldn't keep the horse up all night working on a laptop, staring at a screen. You wouldn't want it to stay indoors with little sunlight, little relaxation or rest, little sleep and on a diet of sugary snacks. And you wouldn't want it racing all day, every day.

You wouldn't demand all of these things of your expensive elite racehorse and then expect that racehorse to perform at its best on race day. You would want your racehorse to be taken care of, fed the most nutritious food, exercised, given the rest it needed and given time in nature. Put very simply, when we feel at our best, we do our best.

If, like I used to, you don't prioritise your own health and mental wellbeing, I urge you to start. You will see immediate and extraordinary gains in mental and emotional energy and clarity when you do – all of which can be fed back into your team to help everyone live and work at their best.

Rest

I often think that building the best version of yourself, and the best school, is a bit like chopping down a tree. If we keep chopping without pause, our axe will get blunt or, worse, break, and so will we. To chop down a tree, we have to put down the axe from time to time to rest. As leaders, this is the equivalent of setting boundaries and giving ourselves time to be a mum, dad, daughter, son or partner. We also have to sharpen our axe, which in our context means being tenacious about upskilling ourselves and continuously learning. This enables us to do our job even better.

Check in with yourself regularly

Finding that work-life balance – or harmony, as I prefer to call it – is possible, but it needs deliberate, conscious attention. Remember that school life is a little like farming; it is seasonal, and there are busier times interspersed with periods that are calmer. These can and should be planned for. The happiest, highest performers in the world regularly spend time planning, intention setting and reflecting to celebrate their wins. I recommend introducing a similar system for yourself. You can make it a daily, monthly, weekly, termly or annual ritual – whatever works best for you.

2. Find something meaningful

Let's travel back in time to 1671, when Christopher Wren observed three bricklayers working away at his rebuilding of St Paul's Cathedral. One was crouched, one was half-standing and the third was standing tall.

Wren approached the crouched bricklayer and asked, 'What are you doing?' He replied, 'I'm a bricklayer and I'm working hard to lay bricks to feed my family.' He asked the same question of the bricklayer who was half-standing. He replied, 'I'm a builder and I'm building a wall.' When Wren asked that question of the third and most productive bricklayer, his response was, 'I am a cathedral builder. I am building a great cathedral to the Almighty.'

This story illustrates the power of having a higher purpose and giving people something meaningful to work towards. When you're building a high-performing team, *give them a cathedral*, so you can all tap into your wonderful uniqueness as a school and relentlessly pursue your core purpose. We've found embedding our core purpose into our vision has been very valuable.

> **Our vision**
>
> At East Wichel, our vision is:
>> To shape aspirational, kind human beings who are equipped for life, passionate and able to make a positive difference in the world.
>
> Stories are an incredibly powerful way to communicate a message so that it really sticks. We created a story of our vision, which you can watch in this video: www.eastwichel.swindon.sch.uk/welcome
>
> It's worth noting that this story was written and shared with the staff team repeatedly during development days, long before it became a reality. We still revisit it now.

3. Clarify your core drivers

Behind our vision are three core drivers. These are the main challenges we feel we want to address in the world. They inform everything we do.

- The first driver is **locality**. As I've said, Swindon has been repeatedly criticised, but heavily criticising a place helps no one. To counter this, we teach the history and culture of our town. Our aim is to build a strong sense of identity, belonging and pride for Swindon and turn those negative narratives around.
- Then we have **humanity**. This one arose from our concerns around rising mental and physical health worries, together with a feeling of growing disconnection within society and from each other as humans, as well as from nature and our planet.
- Our final driver comes from many of the **problems** that are in the world currently that our children are going to need to be able to

solve, such as the fallout from the pandemic, the rise of tech, global warming, poverty and inequality.

These core drivers are threads that are interwoven into every single area of our school, bringing our vision to life.

4. Eliminate wherever you can

Often when we think about improving, we think about doing more. But there is great power in elimination.

Consider how we learn to ride a bike. Bike manufacturers tried adding a handle to the back, which worked for some children but not others. Then they tried adding stabilisers, with the same effect. In the end, the most powerful thing manufacturers did was to get rid of the pedals on the bikes, so the children could push themselves along with their feet. They eliminated something.

So, before we add anything in our school, we always ask ourselves what we can eliminate. We look for anything we feel is not having an impact or is sapping our time. Examples of what we've eliminated include formal lesson observations, distance marking, displays of children's work and the requirement to produce short-term planning documents in generic formats. This is an ongoing process, and we are constantly asking ourselves what impact each action is having.

5. Seek efficiency

We looked at some of the highest performers in the world to learn how they are so efficient – what is it that they do? This led us to develop systems, hacks, routines, rituals and processes for absolutely everything. These reduce workload and enable the organisation to run smoothly, because they free up cognitive bandwidth and the ability to be innovative and creative. This in turn increases capacity, which enables us to move forwards. Our aim is for these systems to be consistent and fully embedded to the point that they become unconscious habits.

We've also found priority matrices are helpful, particularly when someone is feeling overwhelmed. They allow us to identify what are called 'needle movers' – in other words, tasks that are going to move our school forward. The most successful organisations in the world spend

60% of their time on needle movers, which is what we aim for (easier said than done in a school environment). A priority matrix can help us work out what is a needle mover in different situations.

We've also used the Pomodoro Technique, which is a scientifically proven way to improve focus. My senior leaders and I book in 'CEO time', which is when we can have the headspace to think strategically about the school. Ideally, we carve out one to two hours per week for this. Another top tip we would advocate is to schedule *everything* and batch and block tasks as much as possible.

The magical effect of time multipliers

Time multipliers are tasks that will take you time now but will save you time in the future. An example would be putting together an FAQs document for parents, or perhaps recording some short explainer videos that talk about how our systems at the school work. You could use these with parents, new staff or even the children. The exciting thing is, the more time multipliers you find, the more impact they have.

6. Build systems

We have systems for everything, which feeds into our drive for efficiency and eliminating what's unnecessary, helping everyone on our team perform at their best. All our systems are supported by our vision, values and core drivers. Our systems for teaching our behaviour curriculum have been particularly effective.

First, we explicitly teach the behaviour we want to see, narrate the 'why' behind it in the form of a story and use photographs to show the children what good looks like – and, on some occasions, what we don't want to see. We have assembly routines that incorporate our behaviour curriculum, and we provide all our children with tools they can use for self-regulation, such as mindfulness practices and breathing techniques. We've found these not only benefit our pupils, but also our staff.

We've also found that having specific areas for different kinds of self-regulation within classrooms works really well in our school. So, within all our classrooms we think about how to create a calm, neutral environment that minimises cognitive load. Each classroom contains worry boxes, as well as calming stations, affirmation stations and self-regulation areas. We have check-in dolls for the younger children to help them talk about their feelings, and we've heavily invested in books that teach about empathy. In fact, we've found stories are a really powerful tool for changing behaviour, and we've used books to overcome all kinds of behavioural challenges, from biting to swearing.

Second, we have systems for the day-to-day management of behaviour at our school, such as using non-verbal behaviour-management signals. We've found that these reduce cognitive load and also create the calm environment we are striving for to improve everyone's wellbeing.

Third, we have a robust record-keeping system that enables us to track and monitor patterns and trends in behaviour so we can improve it over time.

Finally, we also have clear systems and routines to reward, reflect and repair. The underlying aim of all of these systems is for our children to be kind human beings who can make a difference in the world.

We have also created systems around our curriculum. One that is highly effective is our system for assessment in foundation subjects, which is mindful of both impact and teacher workload. We also have crib sheets and a bank of videos that our teachers can use for what we call automaticity drivers. These are things that enable our children to go to a deeper level of thinking, problem solving and reasoning.

Another system that helps everyone perform at their best is the way in which we highlight examples of good practice. We record any examples of good practice we come across and provide videos to make it easier to share those practices with the whole team.

Putting reading at the heart of our curriculum

We're especially proud of our systems for reading – Ofsted even said we 'went beyond the teaching of reading' at our school.

We have a carefully planned daily story time or book talk session that lasts for 30 minutes every day. We prioritise our professional development around this and give our teachers a lot of support in the area, because we believe it's so key.

> We have also introduced a really strong fairytales thread that runs throughout every year group – in upper key stage 2 those fairytales are in French. Another system we've introduced is our reading canon. Each year group has six books that they read, with a display in each classroom showing the book covers. By the time each child leaves us in Year 6, they will have read 34 novels during their years at our school, which is a fantastic foundation.
>
> We've chosen each book carefully to connect with the core drivers I explained earlier. Another system we use is book hooks, which are displays of objects and other things that help our children create visual patterns of the story they're reading.
>
> But our systems aren't just about encouraging children to read in the classroom. We want them to develop the same love of reading I had as a child, so each child will have their own copy of each novel. We also encourage them to use reading scrapbooks to help develop their passion for reading and stories.

The systems we have in place for our early years teaching are particularly important because these lay the foundations for our children, and they've been instrumental in helping us deal with the high-level challenges we've all seen post-Covid-19. We are Hygge-accredited, which is an approach originating from the Nordic countries that encourages a home-from-home approach, and together with soft lighting, aromatherapy and lots of nature we have created a seasonal curriculum and calm environment that promotes self-regulation.

All of these systems help our team to be the best they possibly can, for themselves and our children.

Building team capacity

Once you have systems in place to support your curriculum, create an efficient environment and encourage positive behaviour in school, it's much easier to focus on building the capacity of your team. In my experience, we rise to the level of the beliefs and expectations we set (often referred to as the Pygmalion Effect), so I urge everyone to treat your team like the hard-working, highly professional and capable human beings that you *want* them to be. I imagine you are doing this already, but could you do it *even* better? I ask myself this often.

Belief is one of the strongest drivers of wellbeing and performance. When you think about it, your team will probably have a collective experience numbering hundreds of years. When you believe in everyone, you can tap into this vast collective knowledge and become stronger together.

The way in which I build capacity in my team – which you may find works for your team – is to adopt the same principle I set out in 'Look after yourself like it's your job' on page 129. I want my team to seek out things that inspire them and make them excited about their roles. I want them to feel fired up and lifted, so I share the steps that have helped me improve my wellbeing and performance with everyone on my team.

Their happiness, their physical and mental health and their overall wellbeing matters to me. I know it affects their performance, but I also know that we only get one life, and I want everyone on my team to live theirs to the fullest.

Building a happy place

The inspectors looked at me. 'Usually when we ask the staff-wellbeing question, we get some uncomfortable shuffling and heads down. We have to say we had to shut your team up. I've never seen a response like it.' I beamed from ear to ear.

How did we get here? We learned from many of the happiest, highest performing teams in the world who have these four things in common:

1. **Autonomy.** Happy teams have a voice: they have a say in how they work and what they work on. I love the principle that people support what *they* create.

2. **Appreciation.** Show you are genuinely grateful for the work your team does. When we feel like we're appreciated, we want to give more, do more and be more. Ideally, you should build a culture where your team show appreciation for each other and celebrate each other and their unique talents. Our school staff work so incredibly hard. I think sometimes they don't get the recognition that they rightly deserve.

3. **Mastery.** Happy, high-performing teams *feel* like they are improving. So as a leader, make sure you highlight and celebrate those small wins along the way to make these visible to all and provide lots of opportunities for further learning and further growth.
4. **Purpose.** The happiest, highest performing teams in the world feel like they are doing meaningful work and making a difference in the world.

You can't go far wrong by embedding these four principles with your team. In doing so, we eliminated a lot of things that were taking up a huge amount of the team's time, but were having very little impact, as I explained when I talked about needle-moving activities.

But we also focused somewhat relentlessly on building a happy place. Our school environment is beautiful. We wanted to build a place where staff want to come to work and children love to be. We wanted to build a curriculum teachers love to teach and children love to learn. Often, as human beings, we think it is success that leads to happiness, but there is an increasing body of evidence to suggest that it is in fact happiness that leads to success.

Happiness and wellbeing

Happiness and wellbeing are the secret weapons in turbocharging high performance. In many ways, I think of happiness as the WD-40 of a high-performing team. For those who don't know, WD-40 is a lubricant for mechanical parts, and I believe happiness acts like lubricant for your brain. When we feel happy, this releases 'happy hormones' such as serotonin and oxytocin, which make it easier for us to focus, be more productive, work collaboratively and deal with stress and challenges. These hormones make everything flow more easily, so we can be more creative and innovative. They are the lubricant that allows us to work harder and smarter.

There are two main reasons I believe it's beneficial to focus on improving staff wellbeing:

1. Wellbeing impacts their happiness, and a happy team spreads their happiness to those around them. That means happy children and a happy school.

2. Improved wellbeing leads to higher performance. A team that cares for itself is able to care for others. To be the best version of yourself, you must first look after yourself. You cannot pour from an empty cup.

What we do within the education environment requires an inordinate amount of energy, enthusiasm and positivity. The health and wellbeing of your team is the tectonic plate that everything else in their life is built upon. This includes their performance at work, how they show up for themselves and others, and it also impacts everyone around them. As headteachers we would do well to remember this for ourselves too.

Moving the dial on team wellbeing

It can be easy to think of wellbeing as little add-ons and nice-to-haves. But developing true wellbeing in your team is not about the cakes in the staff room on a Friday – as delicious as they may be! It's not about forced mindfulness or yoga sessions, or wellbeing meetings that consume your time.

Instead, it's about thinking holistically about your unique team, your unique setting and their needs. The biggest gift you can ever give your team is time and the elimination of any systems, processes and workload that do not impact positively on staff or pupil happiness or outcomes. Of course, this also benefits you. I know it isn't always easy to make time for reflection on these areas, but when you are able to prioritise it, the results are more than worth it.

In my experience, one of the biggest challenges in achieving this is balancing individual wellbeing needs against what the school needs at any given time. School life naturally has seasons. These are ebbs and flows in terms of the diversity, type and volume of demands and workload over the course of any given year. There are also challenges that arise along the way.

Finding harmony of some sort can be trying at times, and it's hard to know what is the right thing to do in certain situations. Here are five principles that we have used to guide us on our journey:

1. According to Parkinson's Law, work will expand to fill the available time. Sometimes the kindest thing you can do is to set a deadline.
2. Play the long game. Investing time to get it right today to build something stronger for the future will always pay off.
3. Sometimes you need to put all of your efforts and energies into the crocodile nearest to the canoe.
4. You can never please everyone, but maintaining a courageous and steadfast focus on trying to do what is the right thing on balance is a good place to be.
5. Try to remember that everyone is human first and a professional second. Always listen to your team. I find it's helpful to remember that, as the leader, I only see 10% of the issues, but the team sees 100%.

Focusing on your own and your team's wellbeing and stress management is a game changer for achieving high performance. As we've discussed, positive wellbeing impacts your energy, mood, focus and how you show up for yourself and others.

As we all know, negative wellbeing has the opposite effect. An unhappy team is a low-performing team with low confidence, which is going to do the bare minimum. A stressed team is potentially even worse. Stress can be contagious – some studies back this up.[3] There is evidence that the hormone cortisol emits from our pores and can impact those around us.

The impact is thought to be greater if the status of the stressed individual is higher. As leaders who arguably have the highest status within our schools, if we are stressed, that doesn't just affect us, it affects everyone else in our buildings.

Your teams are also leading their classes, and they have the highest status within their teams. So, their stress is then impacting the children, and no

---

[3] Dimitroff, S. J., Kardan, O., Necka, E. A., Decety, J., Berman, M. G., Norman, G. J. (2017) 'Physiological dynamics of stress contagion'. *Scientific Reports*. July 21;7(1):6168.

one wants stressed children. We all know this will bring a host of other challenges our way very quickly indeed.

With the current recruitment crisis and the challenges we're facing regarding an all-time low in terms of the number of people entering our profession, it is not just logical, but arguably essential to make looking after the teams that we have, their wellbeing and their stress management – as well as our own – a priority. The following are some of the ways in which I've built up my team's wellbeing and helped them become high performing – some of these might be useful in your school as well.

Your role as a leader of a high-performing team

Everything begins with us. We are role models, which is why I have recommended that you look after yourself like it's your job. I've found it particularly helpful to visualise the kind of leader I want to be. Use the prompts I shared earlier in this chapter (see page 129) if you'd also like to try this approach.

I want to stress that this is not about being perfect – we are all human. In fact, vulnerability can be helpful at times. We also shouldn't strive to be like someone else – we have to be our authentic selves. That is our superpower. This all helps us become the best possible role models for our teams. I've found the following principles help me stay on track.

Be visible

I don't mean necessarily being at the gate each day and never getting any of your significant admin tasks done. I mean in the sense of 'knowing thy school'. I do this through being aware of my time management, such as by using the Pomodoro Technique I mentioned earlier.

My Pomodoro timer finishes every 40 minutes, at which point I stop what I'm doing. In this pause, I walk the school and can touch base with the team and the children to cultivate a deep awareness and knowledge of the normal day-to-day practice within my school.

Look for the good

Make a point of looking for small wins and shouting these from the rooftops. Get your megaphone out. Often, we're so tied up in the day-to-day that we don't stop to reflect upon the impact of our work and the significant efforts of the team. As the leader, it is such a privilege to see so many different staff teaching and interacting with the children. Highlighting small wins is an opportunity to share the collective learnings of our teams and best practice. I see this as an affirmation of what we hope to see even more of.

When we look for the good, the good gets better. People are happier when their work is recognised, and what drives human motivation most is seeing progress. These wins build momentum and affirm our belief in further success. In other words, success literally builds more success.

Listen deeply

As mentioned previously, it is thought that as a leader you see approximately 10% of the issues, problems and challenges. However, your team sees 100%, so involve them, no matter what their role. I find it helpful to remind myself that my role is the 'why', not the 'how'. As a result, I constantly seek ways to increase autonomy at our school. As Maxine explains in chapter 5, we have to get good at listening.

Be tenacious

Never forget where you're headed, and why. Be absolutely relentless in the pursuit of the vision for your school. I've learned that a healthy level of challenge inspires and empowers my team to become the very best versions of themselves and to believe in a better future. I prioritise delivering feedback to my team, even if it seems like something that could wait, and when I do so I ensure it is delivered in line with the school's vision and values.

Stress is not always bad

Stress can be helpful and is actually necessary for growth – it's how you view stress that really matters. We can use stress as a tool to drive performance. It can sharpen focus and increase blood flow to the creative-thinking and problem-solving parts of the brain. If we can help our teams to focus on the things they can control, we can collectively develop a solution-focused mindset. This allows us to let go of stress more easily and see challenges through a different lens.

Negativity bias

As schools, we are a beacon of hope for more people than we possibly know, but it can be easy to forget this. This is compounded by the fact that as humans, we have something called the negativity bias. This is our tendency to pay more attention to bad things and overlook good things.

When we zoom in on the things that we can actually impact, we can counter this bias, which is incredibly empowering and liberating. So, support your team to see every obstacle, issue, challenge, worry and problem as an opportunity for growth and learning, so we can get better and be even stronger because of it.

What if someone isn't performing?

Sometimes someone on your team won't be performing up to your expectations, or their potential. In this case, it can be easy to fall into the trap of thinking, 'I need to move this person on.'

I would urge a different path, and instead advise loving, nurturing and working with the team you already have. Perhaps you consider me naive, but it is my fervent belief that anyone who enters our profession does so with a big heart and the very best intentions. Life happens, challenges arise and somewhere along the journey many school staff can understandably lose hope and their way.

When this happens, ask yourself what opportunity is in front of you. If you wanted to help turn their performance around, what could you do? What would need to happen? If you were successful, how would that make them feel? How would it make you feel? I have found these reflective questions invaluable in my time as a headteacher.

I take enormous pleasure and pride in making it my personal mission to inspire and reignite a passion and a love for what we do in these individuals. The work that school staff do is so incredibly noble and potentially life-changing for individuals and for society, as well as for themselves. There are few things in life that bring me as much joy as seeing that transformation. Many of these staff go on to become very strong in their fields. And let's face it, in the current recruitment crisis, inspiring people makes sense!

Change is the only constant

I like to think that maintaining team performance is like tending to a large country garden. It requires relentless attention, love and care by a hardworking and committed group of people to produce a thing of true, lasting beauty and prevent the weeds from overrunning. Complacency has a tendency to creep up on us all unless it's kept in check.

What is tricky is noticing the gradual changes that happen over time. We can be so immersed in our school environment that we don't necessarily notice changes until they create problems. Keeping on top of these incremental changes, which can lead to a decline in standards (even if it's only small), expectations and achievements is, I believe, one of our biggest challenges as headteachers.

However, I take comfort in knowing this is a natural and normal process in not only schools, but life as a whole. Once I realised this, I was able to anticipate it. One of the most helpful things to remember is that change is the only constant. Keeping this front of mind helps me to continually reflect, learn, grow, innovate and create to ensure we evolve and keep moving forwards.

As backwards as it may sound, I've found it helps to plan and prepare for this decline, knowing that it's heading my way. This approach is based on a principle called the Stockdale Paradox.[4] Confront the brutal facts of the current reality in your schools but maintain a relentless hope and passion for the future, knowing that you and your team will prevail in the years ahead.

We all know that building an exceptional school is not a destination; it's a journey, and it's this ongoing process that makes what we do so meaningful and fulfilling.

We also need to be mindful that landscapes change. New staff members and cohorts bring fresh challenges as well as opportunities, and we must adapt to these. There can be political and societal changes that also require adaptation, such as the rise in tech, inequality across the globe and climate change, to name but a few. These external challenges bring

---

4   Jim Collins, Concepts – 'The Stockdale Paradox' (no date). https://www.jimcollins.com/concepts/Stockdale-Concept.html

a new dimension to our work that must be acknowledged and responded to if we are to continue to move forward.

My advice is to focus on the things we can control, for example our efforts, our attitude, our actions and our energy. We cannot control the many changes that come our way or the circumstances, but we can always control how we view and respond to them.

In my school, we are a strong, happy and united team, and we genuinely care for each other. So when several incredible individuals relocated and had to move on from the school, we were bereft. They had been strong, dynamic and pioneering within their roles in the organisation. How would we continue our current trajectory without these key individuals?

Although our hearts felt differently, experience told us the team and the vision would prevail, because no individual *is* that team – not even me as the leader. It's not about filling anyone's shoes – that's impossible. Everyone is wonderfully unique and brings their own special viewpoints, talents, skills and pure joy to the team. So I changed my perspective. The change in staff presented us with new challenges, but also with a whole new set of opportunities for growth.

Our aim at East Wichel is to build something special, something that is here long after we are all gone, a legacy that we leave behind. So we are constantly fostering and growing our own – the next 'Team 2.0'. We show up and we do our best every day. We care for each other every day. We stay open and humble every day. These are our mantras.

We make a difference, and we continue to grow into the very best versions of ourselves for the children, for each other and for our community. This, I believe, is the essence of a high-performing team.

> **TOP TIPS**
>
> * Look after yourself like it's your job and encourage your team to do the same. Feel free to use some of my suggestions or find whatever works to enhance your own wellbeing.
> * Reflect on what kind of leader you want to be and model this at every available opportunity.
> * Plan for an inevitable decline in standards – even if it's only small. When we accept that there is a natural cycle of change in our schools, we can be mindful and catch any sign of decline, steering us quickly back towards 'outstanding'.

Chapter 8:
Nurturing an exceptional school culture – Ian Scotchbrook

Meet Ian...

Ian Scotchbrook is the headteacher at South Harringay Schools. In 2011, Ian became the head of South Harringay Junior School, which federated with South Harringay Infant School five years later – a process that Ian admits felt like bridging a huge divide at the time. Ian and his team are united around a shared vision and ethos, which enables them to deliver a high-quality education to children across the board. This approach also led to South Harringay Junior School being graded as 'outstanding' by Ofsted in 2023.

About South Harringay Junior School

	School	National average
Pupils with a SEND Education, Health and Care Plan	1.4%	2.5%
Pupils with SEND support	16.7%	13.5%
Pupils whose first language is not English	35.2%	22.0%
Pupils eligible for free school meals at any time during the past six years	17.6%	25.9%

When I started as headteacher at South Harringay Junior School, I had little idea of where my journey would take me. It was my first headship, and I came into a school that I would describe as 'rather basic and sketchy', which was also an accurate description of our school logo at that point! The school had just scraped satisfactory in its latest Ofsted inspection, the outcomes were poor and we had a deficit of a little over £250,000.

On the other side of the fence, with just a narrow passage separating us, was South Harringay Infant School and Ladder Children's Centre. They were different from us in so many ways – they had a lot more money and knew how to spend it, for starters. We would peer over the fence, and I admit to feeling jealous of their situation. It was as though we were the poor cousins of the family. They had been rated 'outstanding' by Ofsted, although their outcomes had slipped since the inspection and we all knew they wouldn't keep that rating the next time the inspectors came round.

When we federated five years later, I felt like bridging the gap between our schools was like crossing the Grand Canyon. It felt like we were worlds apart. But what I and my teams in both schools realised was that we had more in common than we thought, and by working together and listening across the divide we were able to nurture an exceptional school culture that serves us and our pupils well to this day.

I freely admit that we're magpies and have begged, borrowed and stolen examples of best practice from other schools, always giving credit where it's due. I'd be honoured if you were to take that approach to what I share here too. Take whatever you feel could help you to nurture your school's culture from what I explore in this chapter.

The road to federation

In 2011, Michael Gove was in his academisation heyday and our school, as well as the one next door, was among those he'd singled out in Haringey to become academies. Back then, it didn't happen – I only learned of the proposal once I was in post. So I got stuck into my work at South Harringay Junior School as a new headteacher. Gradually our situation began to improve, and we started to align a little more with our neighbours. We even had a new logo designed that matched up with that of the infant school (courtesy of the same parent who had designed theirs). We were feeling less like the poor cousin already.

Then, in 2015, the headteacher of the infant school left and the board of governors returned to the idea of federation. We underwent a full consultation, and in 2016 the infant and junior schools took the leap and federated. I became acting head in the first year and was appointed substantive head thereafter.

My challenge was how to create a whole school from what felt like two separate entities. Even though we lived next to each other, we were doing separate things and the schools felt quite different. My remit was to seek out the opportunities for growth and change that would bring us all together.

Finding a happy path

While it would have been easy to focus on the more pragmatic aspects of our schools, such as exams, tests and curriculum creation, I knew this wouldn't create the happy, welcoming culture and community I wanted. I knew that without a strong culture, we would only get so far.

When there are 'pragmatic problems' shouting for your attention, putting your focus on culture can be easier said than done, but all I can tell you is that in my experience it is worthwhile spending time on creating, sustaining and nurturing a truly exceptional culture on your journey to 'outstanding'.

At South Harringay, we started by thinking about what sorts of behaviours, attitudes and ideas needed to be created, cultivated and nurtured. This wasn't a 'once and done' job; it's thinking that is sustained over time so that our children get the best experience possible.

I believe pupils' experiences should not only value the more obvious aspects of education, like exam results and knowledge acquisition, which are fundamental and important, but also help them understand how their actions, beliefs and attitudes contribute to creating a community and a place of belonging.

We all know this is a vital part of schooling, especially considering how fractious and challenging society can be, how polarised we're becoming on a range of issues and how many children and young adults are becoming isolated in terms of their behaviour and interactions.

Our intention at South Harringay is to give them a sense in school that, if they engage together on a common purpose and a common set of rules and ideas about behaviour and attitudes, their lives can be much richer, as can the lives of those around them. This, I believe, is a fundamental part of what we do as school leaders.

But where do you start on delivering on those ambitions, especially in a newly federated school? We decided to focus first on ensuring all children feel safe, happy and are learning well in all areas, and that all of our staff feel the same way. I appreciate this may sound obvious, but in my experience these 'soft' sides of education can sometimes be overlooked – after all, they're not measured in the same way as academic performance is.

As Paula explains in chapter 7, as headteachers we need all of our staff, teachers, teaching assistants, admin team and everyone else to feel safe and happy so that they can teach well and provide all the services they do effectively. We realised that by creating this healthy environment for our team, we could ensure our children have a positive experience in every part of their education. I'm sure this is also what you're striving for in your school.

For our children to feel safe and happy, and learn well, they need the staff, the adults around them and the other children to behave in ways that lead to this outcome. We agreed that what we do with each other and to each other should ultimately come back to that one goal: that everyone feels positive and is learning or doing their job well.

This was the ethos we followed when navigating the early stages of our federation, and it's one that has underscored our school culture ever since.

Nurturing an exceptional school culture – with feeling

The work we've done with Sonia and her team at Heads Up has been instrumental in tipping us from good into exceptional – or as we call ourselves, 'marvellous and fantastic'. We like to use adjectives that don't usually appear in Ofsted reports to describe our school.

What has been particularly important is being given the tools, space and time to do the deep thinking we needed to do in order to achieve an exceptional school culture. As you've heard from many of the contributors to this book, focusing on a school's vision and values is pivotal for succeeding on the journey to 'outstanding'.

We worked closely with Sonia to create our school vision because we realised that although we had a vision and values already, no one really understood or *felt* them. This meant they weren't having the intended effect. What follows is our school vision. I feel fantastic every time I read this, which is the kind of feeling we want everyone to have when they read our vision.

> Our school is a thriving village ready to welcome those who have travelled from near and far and need a place to belong.
>
> Our village welcomes all people, and those who struggle to feel at home will be enveloped within our heart, because time and care is taken to support those first tentative steps and each individual journey.
>
> As village elders, we're excited by the variety that village life brings. We try to make every day better than the last.
>
> We prepare our people for their time when they will join another village, or even create their own.

We regularly revisit our vision, and it really does run through every part of our school. While Ofsted and their opinions aren't the be all and end all, I was particularly proud to see our school described as 'a thriving village' in one report. Our school does what it says on the tin.

When we were reimagining our vision, we not only wanted it to describe who we are, but also to remind us about who we need to and aspire to be.

Our values do the same. We whittled these down from seven to four, because we wanted to make sure that our children and our staff could really understand what each one means and how they are significant for them. Our values are:

- Resilience.
- Honesty.
- Contribute.
- Respect.

We share our values and what they mean in a variety of ways, ranging from songs and stories to poetry and themed assemblies. We are also very clear about what each of these values looks like in terms of the outcomes and behaviours we want to see.

> **From seed to tree**
>
> To bring these concepts to life for our children and help them understand what each value looks like for them, we've used the analogy of a tree. So the behaviours and outcomes we look for are broken down into three stages: seed, sapling and tree.
>
> Each stage represents where that child is on their journey to fully embodying each of our values. For example, the seed stage of 'Respect' includes the outcome, 'Actively listen to others'. In the sapling stage, we have, 'Speak to everyone calmly and politely'. Finally, in the tree stage, we have, 'Know when it is appropriate to speak'.
>
> Our values are discussed in these terms with our children regularly, so they not only understand our school values but have time to embed them and evaluate each other and themselves in relation to how they're exhibiting those behaviours. The lesson for us was that unless you can see, hear and feel every value, they are a little pointless.
>
> But when you can plant a value, like a seed, in children at the start of their journeys, you can see them grow and watch as they drive your culture forward.

A values-based approach to people and performance appraisals

We've also taken our list of behaviours that are attached to each value and integrated them into the discussions we have as part of performance appraisals with our team. I feel it's important to point out here that none of us fully embody every value all day, every day. We're all human and we all have off days. I've found it really important to be vulnerable with my staff when it's appropriate, and to let them know if I've had a week where I perhaps haven't exhibited all the desirable outcomes associated with one of our values consistently.

This means we have honest discussions about our performance at every level, and in doing so everyone develops more leadership capacity. We're very clear in defining all our teachers as leaders, because that's what they are. We not only make this clear within our internal documentation, but we also use that language throughout the recruitment process.

We've even developed a document that sets out our core teaching standards in such a way that it demonstrates what leadership looks like on every stage of their journey, from the start of the main pay scale all the way up to the top of the upper pay scale. However, this isn't a document that sits on a desktop, never to see the light of day. We encourage all of our teachers to regularly assess and evaluate themselves against those standards. This helps them to prepare for performance appraisals and ensures we have productive conversations.

These documents are different depending on each person's role in the school, so in the performance appraisal document for middle leaders, for example, there is more of a focus on leadership specifically. Our aim with these tools is to help each member of our team to think about their various responsibilities and what kind of behaviour we are expecting to see from them as they progress within the school.

We've also refined the system for having performance appraisals. We now call them development conversations, and, like many of you reading this, we have these conversations in the autumn term. Each teacher is given a one-page document to fill in before their development planning meeting. This document encourages them to evaluate themselves against the core teaching standards we've set out. It's an opportunity for each individual to highlight their strengths as well as their own areas for improvement in relation to our school values.

During those development conversations, we encourage each person to isolate an area within one of those values that they want to focus on over the coming school year. We make notes in their performance appraisal document, but we keep these short and punchy. We also have 10-minute check-ins throughout the rest of the school year to assess progress. Any notes made in these check-ins are kept to a minimum – the aim is that each person's document is no more than two pages long by the end of the year.

We've found that taking a more collaborative approach to performance appraisals has made them feel more alive and more meaningful for all of our teachers. In fact, our teachers like this approach so much that at the time of publication we are in the process of rolling it out for our teaching assistants as well.

The feedback I've had from my team is that this approach allows them to take ownership of their performance and professional development, and they're really positive about the new collaborative nature of these conversations.

Celebrating each other and our contributions

As well as focusing on our values and ensuring everyone understands what we mean by each value, we make sure that we also celebrate successes around all these values.

Each year we come together as a team to refresh our understanding of our values. One year it may be enough to think about resilience in terms of picking oneself up when things are tough; the following year it may need to be aligned with a school improvement priority around our learning in art, so we focus more on resilience when being creative, for example.

We're always striving to deepen our understanding around our cultural ecosystem, which encompasses the values and the vision. That means we're always reviewing, revising and improving that ecosystem – in other words, we're nurturing it. For example, we've deepened our understanding of our value of contribution and allowed people a greater scope to explore what they could contribute to the school in a multitude of ways.

That contribution could simply be showing recognition of someone else, ensuring they don't feel isolated or overwhelmed, or making a contribution to somebody else's mental wellbeing.

An example of such behaviour is teachers and support staff checking in and asking how I am during a particularly trying period. As I'm sure you know, it can feel a little lonely when you're a headteacher, because you're constantly thinking about other people's wellbeing and the wellbeing of the organisation itself, as well as all the individuals in it. However, that doesn't necessarily mean others think about you.

Having other members of staff check in with me was a very reassuring and unexpected surprise. It's now become part of our practice, all because we've nurtured our culture by exploring those values at a deeper level in an incremental way.

We've had a number of key staff members, particularly at the support staff level, who have come forward to provide contributions to the pastoral and wider curriculum too. One employee recently revealed that they are an ex-champion tap dancer and are keen to share that particular skill. We're in the process of introducing tap lessons as I write this now. Tap dancing is not something I ever would have considered offering as part of our school programme, but it's quite exciting to have the opportunity to introduce it!

That deep examination of our school values and its instant contribution has allowed people to see a variety of ways in which they can contribute to our culture, from small acts like checking in on everybody to make sure they're okay, to offering to share a particular skill they have for the benefit of others.

The key principle I hope you take from this is that aligning your people with your culture can open up whole layers of support you were previously unaware of that could make your school an even better place – you may also have a former champion in your midst. Just imagine how you could strengthen your community by regularly tending to that cultural ecosystem and thinking about why those particular mechanisms, concepts and values you have in your school are in place. My advice is to keep encouraging everyone to ask what else you could do.

Measuring up

The difficulty with steering a cultural change and then maintaining an exceptional culture is that measuring the cultural shifts is not a straightforward quantitative analysis. You're not looking necessarily at numbers, test scores or progress rates in the way that we're used to doing with some of the more obvious things in education like test results.

But I knew that I didn't want to leave the cultural impact to chance, so I decided I would find a way to formulate and carefully plan how we could measure our culture's growth and impact. Hopefully some of the ways in which we've done this may help you if this is an area you're also finding challenging.

Quite quickly we realised that in order to demonstrate cultural impact, we needed to measure behaviours over time. Naturally there will be an element of perception and subjectivity to those judgements, but that doesn't mean that you can't take the behaviours seriously and plan for them.

The key is to carefully consider what behaviours you want to measure in your school to track your cultural impact, and then think about how you can build in regular opportunities for that measurement to happen.

As a senior leadership team, we regularly think about each member of our team not just in terms of their teaching skills but also their willingness to engage fully with the culture of the school. We do this as a group so there are a variety of perspectives involved. We've all agreed that this measurement doesn't need to be precise; it's simply a way of gauging where we are as a team. More importantly, we can then think about what we're going to do to support those who may not be as engaged as we would like them to be.

This support could come from a range of measures, such as providing mentoring experience. One way in which we've introduced this at our school is to pair up any staff member who needs some support with someone who is showing real willingness to participate within the culture of the school.

We also regularly measure ourselves against various aspects of our cultural ecosystem, whether it be teaching and learning, behaviour and attitude or children and staff. To do this, we rate ourselves from 1 to 10 against the objectives we want to achieve and the behaviours we want to see, hear and feel underneath each of those headings. These categories are our markers of success.

We revisit this every couple of years because, of course, every couple of years we have made progress, which is always exciting to see. This exercise also allows us to increase our expectations over time. Perhaps a behaviour that was previously number eight in a particular category has now moved up to six or seven, for example. As a team, we can then ask what needs to happen to move it up again.

Putting yourself in the cultural driving seat

I can't overstate the importance of measuring the impact over time of the culture you are building. This is vital for sustaining and nurturing it. If you don't make a concerted effort to measure the impact, you're not allowing yourself the opportunity to evaluate the work that you've put in – and often you will have put in a lot of work, which deserves to be celebrated.

When we don't measure our efforts, we're also in danger of allowing what could be a really exciting and dynamic cultural journey to plateau or wither. As education professionals, we all know the value of benchmarks and regular testing. We have to apply this approach to our culture if we want to see the impact we're having and ensure it's our intended impact.

We need this assessment to put ourselves in the driving seat of our schools' cultural transformations. Without it, we can't navigate our cultural transformation effectively. We're drifting, leaving our organisations open to the whims of all those various external and internal complications and pressures that can buffet a school and drag it in a particular direction, risking taking it off its cultural course.

While our opinion and assessment of our schools' culture and performance as headteachers is vital, we are not the only ones who can assess and help nurture a school's culture. In my experience, getting external perspectives is just as important as listening to internal ones.

Looking in from the outside

One of the main challenges in measuring cultural impact within our schools is often that we're too close to the culture to measure certain impacts. It may also be that we don't trust our own judgements to be as precise as they could be. However, there are opportunities to step back and assess our culture from outside.

In our school, we've invited trusted external individuals to assist us in making those judgements. We've learned that trusted governors can often be a good source of information. They approach the situation with a fresh set of eyes and have listened to the intent of your culture at various meetings. This allows them to contribute evidence for judgements that you're trying to make.

A trusted local authority representative or any other external person can also provide a useful perspective. We've worked closely with Sonia and Heads Up, and I'll talk more about the impact their input has had shortly. But we also work with the Haringey Education Partnership (HEP), which was established when the school improvement facility was taken out of local authority control. The Haringey schools didn't want to lose their collegiate approach, so HEP was set up to provide school improvement services. It's run by headteachers, for headteachers, and it's fantastic.

Of the 120 HEP member schools, 97% are rated as 'good' or 'outstanding' by Ofsted (at the time of publication).

The most important caveats to bringing in someone external are to know that they will give you an honest answer and have some understanding of what you're trying to achieve as a school. When you can tick these two boxes, this external input can only add value, supporting you in understanding what your culture is doing and how it's evolving.

Another valuable external perspective can come from regular visitors. For our school, this often includes prospective parents visiting in the autumn term to look for a Reception place for their child for the following year. After one parent tour, a father approached me to ask if everything he'd seen was just put on for the tour's benefit. When I assured him this was how our school looked on a regular day, he was blown away.

These parents usually have probing questions and appreciate honesty and transparency. I often highlight our cultural initiatives and major school improvement items, asking them to look for evidence of these during their tour.

For example, when our junior and infant schools federated several years ago, we aimed to create a cohesive cultural environment. I would highlight this to visiting parents and ask them to assess whether the school felt cohesive. Did they sense a curriculum flow from Reception to Year 6? Did the separate buildings feel like the same school?

This approach often yields positive feedback. We also make our school's vision clear – to create a welcoming village where everyone belongs – and ask visitors to look for evidence of this. Even when I forget to mention this, prospective parents often tell us they see the school as a welcoming village.

Other external individuals, such as supply teachers, can also provide unique insights into your cultural impact. Even those in for just a day can share how they were treated and whether your cultural values were extended to them. If a supply teacher is with us for a longer period, we ask them to not only evaluate our culture but to contribute to it.

Shutting down the inner demons

I don't know about you, but as a headteacher I often focus on all there is still to do. I'm not always great at looking at where we started and what we've achieved. The inner demons in my head are constantly whispering, *It's not finished. It's not done. It's not perfect.* The truth is this work will never be 'done', and I'm beginning to accept that.

One school improvement partner in particular helped me to see just how far we'd come. They pointed out to me that, based on what they were seeing in some of the other schools they visited, we were selling ourselves a bit short. 'Your school has got to a point where it is truly special, so feel good about that. Feel proud about that.' This stopped my inner demons dead. For the first time, I really listened and heard what other people thought of our school, and that allowed me to get out of my own way.

We weren't going to rest on our laurels, but for the first time I could really see we were in a place of flow and our journey was going much more smoothly than I thought.

Sustaining an exceptional school culture

I've already talked about the importance of focusing on the behaviours we want to see over time in our schools and tying those back to our vision and values, not only for our children but also our staff. This is how we've merged two schools and created a culture in which everyone's attitudes and beliefs align.

Throughout this process at South Harringay Schools, I found it helpful to reflect on the following questions:

- What kind of emotions do you want the people within your school to have as they engage with each other or as they finish their school day?
- What kind of responses do you want them to show towards each other when they're having a bad day?

This concept can be applied to any organisation or microculture – even to your own home. Applying this on a grander scale, to the school, helps to hone the full range of behaviours you see now, as well as the optimum behaviours you want to encourage to create the environment you desire over time.

Although this can feel like a lot to do when you're just setting off on this journey, I can assure you it isn't hard work once you have clarity from your cultural ecosystem and you really know who you are as a school. Once you achieve this cultural clarity, you can do a little bit regularly and often, and these little bits are very easy to implement.

The little bits can be as simple as walking around the school in the morning and chatting to staff, reminding them about a particular value that's in place or praising them for something they've done that demonstrates that value. You could let them know how much you appreciate the fact their environment is supporting the school's vision. I've learned the key is inserting those little things quite explicitly.

Other ways I reinforce our culture include:

- As we have the vision that our school is seen as a welcoming village, I open the emails I write to the staff with, 'Dear villagers'.

- In each staff meeting, I make sure I have the website open on the page that exemplifies the aspect of our culture I want to focus on in that meeting. I then explain why I have chosen that picture and how it relates to that aspect and the meeting.

In other words, this is about looking for every opportunity you can to meaningfully praise the optimum behaviours you've identified, while alluding back to how that behaviour specifically feeds into what we want to hear and feel from each other throughout the school.

It almost becomes a self-fulfilling prophecy because the more you do it, the more examples there are in front of you. After a time, these examples will just seem to present themselves, provided you keep your eyes open. The key, as I mentioned, is looking for and praising behaviour little and often. When you do this, it doesn't feel like work and you'll find your school culture takes on a life of its own.

Keeping your eyes open each day will allow you to filter for the cultural points that you want to see in your school, looking for those behaviours, highlighting and celebrating them and then thinking about how they can be embedded further. We always need to ask ourselves how else we can deepen that particular work.

Staying the course to nurture an exceptional culture

One of the significant challenges to creating and then maintaining an exceptional school environment is the multitude of directives, suggestions and guidance that comes at the school from various sources such as the DfE, Ofsted, local authority, parents and carers. This naturally pulls the school in different directions according to various expectations.

Additionally, there is the internal pressure to adapt to changing demographics and the evolving ethnic makeup of the school. These dynamic factors present challenges at different times. As you well know, all of this needs to be taken into account so you can stay the course and continue to nurture a consistent and strong school culture.

To help us remain on course, the goal I've set for us is to stay true to our school culture while allowing enough flexibility to respond to necessary directives or guidance. These can then be synthesised into our culture in a way that works for us and stays true to our beliefs, values and vision, or to ensure our culture is flexible enough to adapt without compromising our core principles.

This means there's never a time when I'm not nurturing our school culture. It's a constant endeavour that requires systems and processes to ensure its regular nurturing. However, I had to focus on it distinctly during the Covid-19 pandemic period.

Our lives were thrown into chaos, particularly the life of the school – I don't need to tell you that. Not only were all our routines disrupted, but we were called on to act in extraordinary ways for our children and community as we became a repository for the children of key workers.

The challenges of ensuring we were able to serve all children as quickly and efficiently as possible meant a lot of logistics and thought needed to go into how to roll out remote learning, a challenge we all faced. But to do that in isolation from thinking about what it meant to our culture would have been a mistake. We had to think about our values first.

In particular, we have the values of resilience and contribution. We decided to clearly state that we were all going to have to draw on our reserves of resilience and contribute to each other's resilience. I communicated this to staff in remote staff meetings and whenever I got the opportunity to see people face to face.

More than ever, the values and vision of the school became something that could really feed and support our families who were going through a tough time. We were led by our vision and values and ensured that all of our children's needs were met to the best of our ability despite all those challenges. We served our community incredibly well and got excellent feedback for the way we responded to the Covid-19 pandemic. The impact of nurturing that culture was clear and evident not only throughout that period, but also afterwards.

We also took the opportunity to share the success stories we received or were part of. I would share with the staff the very positive emails and phone calls that I got from parents about what we were doing.

All that made us feel very good, as well as professionally and morally satisfied. So, it's often in those times of crisis that you've got to really think about what culture you have in place, and what elements of that culture you're going to emphasise, draw upon and develop to get you through a difficult time.

Transforming a school into a village

When you have a very long list of things to focus on, which we all do as headteachers, I know how easy it can be to want to focus on the pragmatic, logical tasks, but what I hope you can see from what I've shared here is that focusing on culture first will lead to the tangible results you want to see elsewhere.

As you can see from our demographics, and as you've heard from the story about when we federated, our road to an exceptional school culture hasn't always been smooth, and it's still something we have to work on every day.

But as a result of transforming our school into a village, this is not a task I have to do alone. I'm proud to see the impact this has had on our pupils, staff and parents. I've found the sense of being part of a village is particularly obvious when we welcome children from abroad, sometimes from very difficult circumstances. We've had some children join our school from Ukraine, for example.

I've seen each one of these children be embraced by our village community and given a sense of belonging that allows them to achieve, feel happy and be part of the village. In a broader sense, this feeling of community shows up in other places, such as our good attendance record among our pupils, because our children enjoy being at school. Knowing that our children want to be at school and enjoy the relationships they form with each other and the staff gives me immense pleasure.

I'm also always delighted when parents express that they feel their children belong and are safe, which is feedback I regularly receive. We try to make the parents feel that they belong too, while also ensuring that they understand that part of our culture is allowing the professionals to do their jobs. I believe this benefits all of us.

Our culture also impacts staff recruitment and retention. When we recruit, we ensure that our advertisements reflect our school culture. We also focus on professional development, as I've explained, and we carve out the time to nurture our staff to understand and become a part of our culture. While I appreciate this can feel like additional work, we have seen the immense value of doing that work, primarily through staff members staying with us for long periods – something I know we all strive for in the current climate, where recruitment can be a challenge to say the least.

That said, there will always be occasions when members of staff decide to move on, usually because they've reached a stage in their life where they can't meet the demands of our culture. We respect their decision and wish them well in finding an organisation that better suits their needs.

These are just some of the ways in which I've seen having an exceptional school culture feeds into the success and wellbeing of students, parents and staff – and of course you've already read many other examples from the other headteachers who have contributed to this book. But there is one other benefit to focusing on school culture that I have personally experienced…

Love what you do

On a very personal level, I've found creating a high-impact culture and maintaining and nurturing that culture has brought great enjoyment, leading to a greater sense of job satisfaction and professional fulfilment.

Even before I focused on culture, I enjoyed my job, but it has become even more enjoyable since I've developed a culture that has elevated our school to a level we previously couldn't achieve. Despite our best efforts, we never quite reached the level we wanted, not just by external judgements like Ofsted's, but by our own standards.

There was always a sense that we needed to do 'more', and it wasn't until we focused on culture that I grasped what that 'more' was. I'm sure that I'm not alone in having felt like this as a headteacher.

It was only when we focused on our true purpose, aims, and desires for our organisation, and implemented the systems and processes to maintain that culture, that I found the level of job satisfaction I now have and created the exciting and marvellous school I currently work in.

As you'll now know from reading this book, there are many elements that feed into a strong cultural ecosystem within schools. Here are my key takeaways for nurturing a positive culture and encouraging everyone in your community to contribute to it.

> **TOP TIPS**
>
> ★ Focus on the behaviours you want to see as part of your culture and find a way to articulate and bring them to life for everyone. We've found using our values to anchor the behaviours we want to see has been particularly beneficial for students and staff alike.
> ★ Celebrate one another and the contributions you all make to your unique culture. Praise people for acts, big or small, that align with your values.
> ★ Develop a way to measure the impact your culture is having on your school. Accept that this will necessarily be subjective, but seek opportunities to bring in as many perspectives as you can, including those of trusted external observers.

The common thread of culture

When considering what nurturing a school culture looks like beyond my organisation, I reflect on several schools I've worked with professionally through Heads Up. These schools share a common thread: a clear cultural ecosystem that's been thoughtfully and purposefully created and nurtured.

It is evident during visits that the strong leadership within the culture is instrumental in not only creating but also developing that culture. The senior leadership team ensures all opportunities are taken to deepen, strengthen and celebrate it. There's a palpable sense of joy in each school, despite their varying visions, values and contexts.

What remains consistent is a well-defined cultural experience that all staff, pupils and the wider community enjoy and benefit from. This culture manifests itself in many ways, including the environment and how well it's cared for and the alignment between the children's behaviour and attitudes.

It's also evident in the way children of all ages talk about their experience of being in the schools, which is mirrored by the staff. I feel privileged to have observed a set of schools that have undergone a development programme that's not only helped them create a high-performing culture but also assisted them in nurturing it, constantly evaluating and considering its future direction.

As I mentioned earlier, I've also learned a lot from visiting these schools, and I hope that by reading this book you've also found some useful tips and advice you can bring back to your school.

Conclusion

The world is rapidly changing, and those of us working in education are under greater pressure than ever before. But all of us got into education with a passion for helping to shape the next generation and a desire to equip our pupils with the life skills they need to succeed, alongside academic knowledge.

We are no longer just educators – we have to look at the whole life of each child we interact with and work out how to do our best for them. Pupils in school today need to be given the ability to make choices for themselves. The jobs they will be performing as adults may be unimaginable to us now, so we can't teach them job-specific skills with any certainty that they will be useful. But we can help them develop resilience and the ability to cope with change, and provide them with tools to manage and improve their physical, emotional, mental and social wellbeing.

Ultimately, this is what creating an outstanding cultural ecosystem delivers for the children in our care. Throughout this book, you've seen the perspectives of headteachers from many different schools. Each of the headteachers has faced their own challenges, and each of them has successfully found a way through those challenges. But none of them has done so alone. Having a strong team to support you at every level is essential if you want to create a cohesive culture and become an outstanding school in every way.

As you will have realised from reading these stories and perspectives – and as Ian correctly assessed – the common thread between all of the headteachers in shifting their school from good to great is a strong, high-performing school culture that is developed and nurtured to have a lasting positive impact on all who encounter it. What you hold in your hands is a guide, packed with actionable advice from headteachers who understand the struggles you face and have created thriving educational environments. Use whatever you feel is relevant to your school when starting to create a strong cultural ecosystem of your own, to help you find innovative approaches to the challenges you will face and support you in your school's journey to 'outstanding'.

Keep coming back to those three pillars that support a cultural ecosystem – a compelling vision, strong values and clear strategies for building the culture you want to see – and you can't go far wrong. Perhaps most importantly of all, remember that you are not alone on this journey. You not only have the team at your school, but also a network of headteachers who are willing to share what they have learned and experienced with you. You only need to ask. Our hope in writing this book is that headteachers like you are not only inspired to navigate the journey to 'outstanding' successfully but also become aware of the support available to you and your teams to deliver the great education we all want to provide for our children.

What next?

- Are you inspired and wondering where to go from here?
- Are you keen to adopt many of the ideas from these headteachers, but not sure where to start – or want to start everywhere?
- Or are you thinking, 'We're outstanding – woo-hoo!'

Having supported many heads, including many you've met in this book, to navigate their way from good, to great, to greater I have learned the subtle and not so subtle differences between good and great schools.

Learn how your school compares to the ones featured in this book by completing our simple self-assessment tool.

It provides a measure of your school's culture in three vital areas, empowering you to make the changes your school may need. (Only 6% of schools achieve an 'excellent' score in every area…)

Follow the self-assessment link here: outstandingschool.scoreapp.com

- Discover how close your school is to being 'outstanding'.
- Get specific tips to help you close the gap.
- You'll receive your results instantly.
- It takes just 10 minutes.

Sonia Gill

Connect with the authors

Sonia Gill

Sonia Gill helps school leaders to deliver exceptional education for their children. Sonia is the CEO of Heads Up, a qualified teacher and author of two Amazon bestsellers. Since 2011, Sonia has been visiting outstanding schools to uncover what drives their success, to instil those lessons into her leadership training.

X: @SoniaG_HeadsUp

LinkedIn: www.linkedin.com/in/soniagillheadsup/

YouTube: www.youtube.com/@HeadsUpUK

Jo Savidge

Clockhouse Primary School, Clockhouse Lane, Collier Row, Romford, Essex, RM5 3QR

14-15 June 2023 school inspection: Outstanding – files.ofsted.gov.uk/v1/file/50223467

	School	National average
Pupils with a SEND Education, Health and Care Plan	3.1%	2.5%
Pupils with SEND support	8.2%	13.5%
Pupils whose first language is not English	19.2%	22.0%
Pupils eligible for free school meals at any time during the past six years	29.4%	25.9%

X: @ClockhousePrim

Facebook: www.facebook.com/p/Clockhouse-Primary-School-100083006088706/

Helen Nicholson

Stanton School, Bradville, Fairfax, Milton Keynes, Buckinghamshire, MK13 7BE

8-9 December 2021 school inspection: Outstanding – files.ofsted.gov.uk/v1/file/50176783

	School	National average
Pupils with a SEND Education, Health and Care Plan	1.3%	2.5%
Pupils with SEND support	11.9%	13.5%
Pupils whose first language is not English	29.3%	22.0%
Pupils eligible for free school meals at any time during the past six years	41.8%	25.9%

X: @StantonPepper

Paul Murphy

Lancasterian Primary School, King's Road, Tottenham, London, N17 8NN

7-8 June 2023 school inspection: Good – files.ofsted.gov.uk/v1/file/50227870

	School	National average
Pupils with a SEND Education, Health and Care Plan	3.5%	2.5%
Pupils with SEND support	14.8%	13.5%
Pupils whose first language is not English	69.8%	22.0%
Pupils eligible for free school meals at any time during the past six years	47.1%	25.9%

X: @LancasterianPri

Facebook: www.facebook.com/lancsprimary/

Maxine Low

Brooklands Farm Primary School, 152 Fen Street, Brooklands, Milton Keynes, Buckinghamshire, MK10 7EU

29-30 June 2022 school inspection: Outstanding – files.ofsted.gov.uk/v1/file/50193944

	School	National average
Pupils with a SEND Education, Health and Care Plan	1.3%	2.5%
Pupils with SEND support	15.4%	13.5%
Pupils whose first language is not English	53.0%	22.0%
Pupils eligible for free school meals at any time during the past six years	10.2%	25.9%

X: @FarmBrooklands

Facebook: www.facebook.com/profile.php?id=100063518230134&ref=embed_page

Beth Dyer

Nine Acres Primary School, South View, Newport, Isle of Wight, PO30 1QP

10-11 July 2024 school inspection: Outstanding – files.ofsted.gov.uk/v1/file/50256539

	School	National average
Pupils with a SEND Education, Health and Care Plan	3.3%	2.5%
Pupils with SEND support	14.9%	13.5%
Pupils whose first language is not English	6.3%	22.0%
Pupils eligible for free school meals at any time during the past six years	29.1%	25.9%

X: @NineAcresPri

Facebook: www.facebook.com/NineAcresPrimary

Paula Philips

East Wichel Primary School & Nursery, Staldon Road, East Wichel, East Wichel Community Primary School, Staldon Road, Swindon, Wiltshire, SN1 7AG

6-7 December 2022 school inspection: Outstanding – files.ofsted.gov.uk/v1/file/50206071

	School	National average
Pupils with a SEND Education, Health and Care Plan	1.7%	2.5%
Pupils with SEND support	13.1%	13.5%
Pupils whose first language is not English	33.4%	22.0%
Pupils eligible for free school meals at any time during the past six years	14.2%	25.9%

X: @EastWichelSch

Facebook: www.facebook.com/eastwichelprimaryschool/

Ian Scotchbrook

South Harringay Infant and Junior School, Pemberton Road, Haringey, London, N4 1BA

24-25 May 2023 (Infant) school inspection: Good – files.ofsted.gov.uk/v1/file/50222961

24-25 May 2023 (Junior) school inspection: Outstanding – files.ofsted.gov.uk/v1/file/50222917

Infant school

	School	National average
Pupils with a SEND Education, Health and Care Plan	4.7%	2.5%
Pupils with SEND support	4.7%	13.5%
Pupils whose first language is not English	30.2%	22.0%
Pupils eligible for free school meals at any time during the past six years	8.0%	25.9%

Junior school

	School	National average
Pupils with a SEND Education, Health and Care Plan	1.4%	2.5%
Pupils with SEND support	16.7%	13.5%
Pupils whose first language is not English	35.2%	22.0%
Pupils eligible for free school meals at any time during the past six years	17.6%	25.9%

X: @SHJSchool